Sunset

BUILDING birdhouses

EDITED BY DON VANDERVORT AND THE EDITORS OF SUNSET BOOKS

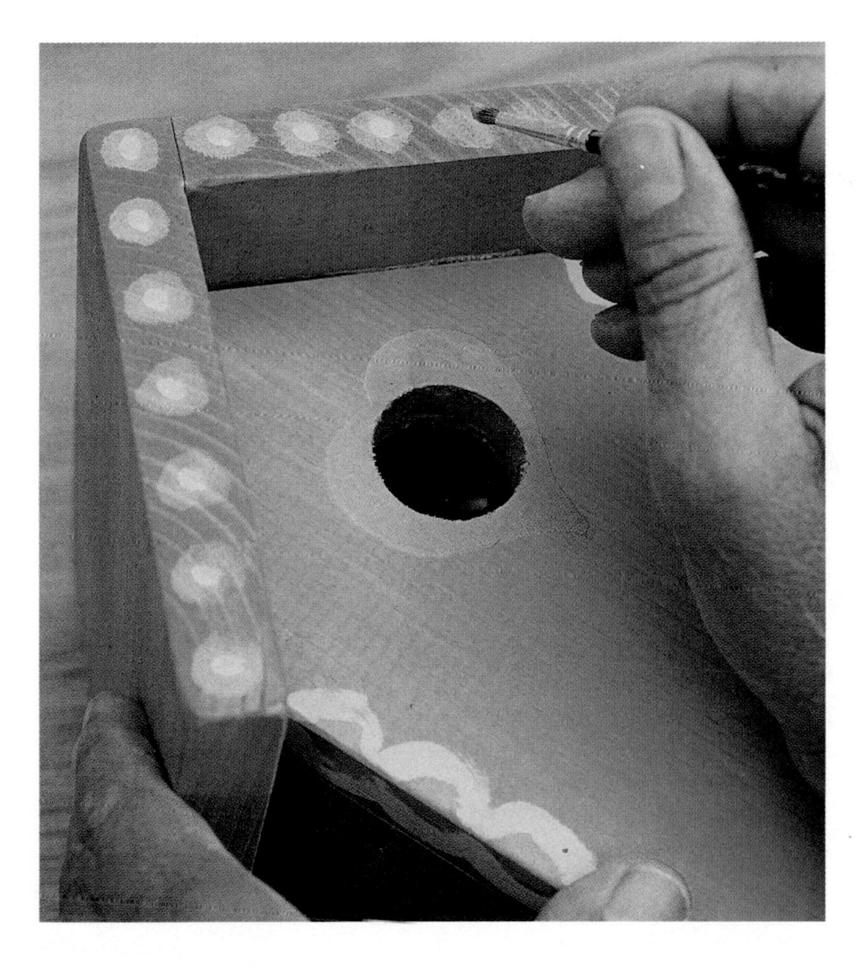

SUNSET BOOKS • MENLO PARK, CALIFORNIA

Sunset Books
VICE PRESIDENT & GENERAL MANAGER: Richard A. Smeby
VICE PRESIDENT & EDITORIAL DIRECTOR: Bob Doyle
PRODUCTION DIRECTOR: Lory Day
ART DIRECTOR: Vasken Guiragossian
DIRECTOR OF OPERATIONS: Rosann Sutherland
SENIOR EDITOR: Marianne Lipanovich

Building Birdhouses was produced in conjunction with HomeTips
EDITOR: Don Vandervort
MANAGING EDITOR: Louise Damberg
PROJECTS DESIGNER & WRITER: Scott Fitzgerrell
ILLUSTRATOR: Melanie Powell, Studio in the Woods
GRAPHIC DESIGNER: Dan Nadeau
BOOK DESIGNER: Harry Kerker
GRAPHIC ASSISTANT: Robin Ireland
CONTRIBUTING EDITOR: Carol Crotta
RESEARCHER: Shelley Ring Diamond
PRODUCTION COORDINATOR: Danielle Javier
PROOFREADER: Lisa Black
EDITORIAL ASSISTANT: Kit Vandervort

COVER DESIGN: Vasken Guiragossian
COVER PHOTOGRAPHY: Norman A. Plate
COVER STYLING: Cynthia Del Fava

10 9 8 7 6 5 4 3 2 1
First Printing June 2002
 Library of Congress Control Number: 2001098578. ISBN 0-376-01035-5. Printed in the United States.

For additional copies of *Building Birdhouses*
or any other Sunset book, call 1-800-526-5111
or visit us at www.sunsetbooks.com.

Contents

Birdhouse building is an ancient art that has remarkably enduring appeal. Even the Romans understood what we understand today—there is something most satisfying about building a house to attract birds to your yard.

Today, birdhouse building as a craft has evolved into a folk- and fine-art form. A trip to the gift shop or garden design center or a few minutes on the Internet turns up birdhouses in a dizzying array of shapes, sizes, materials, themes, and price ranges. No longer just for birds, birdhouses are fast becoming a unique and often treasured home-design element.

With just a touch of inspiration, hobbyists of even the most modest skills can easily create whimsical, bold, and personalized versions of the simple birdhouse. This book is designed to spark your imagination with many versions of the humble birdhouse, from basic to extravagant. And for 26 projects, you'll find plans, lists of materials and tools, and highly detailed step-by-step instructions.

All of the birdhouses featured in this book's projects are functional—that is, if you follow the instructions precisely, each one can serve as a bird habitat. If form is more important to you than function, however, you can use these plans as a launching pad for your own flights of fancy.

Building Birdhouses

The scene is a classic one: It's a gloomy, rainy Saturday, and the children are about to die from boredom when Mom and Dad usher them into the garage workshop. Dad pulls out the old saw, a well-worn hammer, and a ferocious-looking drill, while Mom produces a jelly jar overflowing with a wild assortment of nails and screws. For the better part of an afternoon, the kids measure and mark (only adults are allowed to use the saw), and hammer and paint until at last—the most beautiful birdhouse in the world.

How many of us recall a scene like this from our childhoods? There is something a bit magical about a birdhouse. Simple in shape and easy to construct, it nevertheless captures our imaginations and sparks our creative juices the way few projects do. For some people, building a birdhouse is the perfect parent-child project—a beloved tradition that forges a bond, creates a shared memory, and serves as a forum for instruction about both birds and the craft itself.

As woodworkers and hobbyists can tell you, however, you don't need to have children around you to savor the pleasures of building a birdhouse. The birdhouse has always been one of the most popular home projects, and it is easy to see why. The basic birdhouse form—a small house with four walls, a floor, a roof, and an entry hole—is beguilingly simple and reassuringly forgiving. Even someone with two left hands, so to speak, can fashion one without great stress or strain. Parts are cheap and easy to come by: bits of scrap wood, some nails and screws, nature's cast-offs. The tools are common—saw, hammer, screwdriver, hand or electric drill, maybe a paintbrush. You don't need a lot of planning, and work time can be minimal; a lazy weekend morning or afternoon will do. Yet the sense of accomplishment and pride can be great, far greater than the effort you'll expend.

Many hobbyists use the simple birdhouse form, or even just the birdhouse concept, as a starting point for creative expression. These people often turn out amazingly artistic, often humorous,

ABOVE: Birdhouses have long since come in from the cold to add whimsical touches to home decor. Graceful limbs of a fancifully painted tree serve as a fitting backdrop to display this charming birdhouse collection.

LEFT: With garden areas often treated as outdoor "rooms," birdhouses can provide a decorative touch, especially when grouped for effect. Bird lovers should note, however, that most cavity nesters are territorial by nature and prefer the solitude of a single house per yard.

OPPOSITE: A birdhouse in progress on a home workbench is a sweetly familiar sight, for good reason. Birdhouse building is one of the easiest and most rewarding crafts for woodworking hobbyists of all ages.

and sometimes downright wild turns on the basic birdhouse.

Just about anything can serve as an inspiration for the birdhouse form—a log cabin or fire station, an old cowboy boot, a devilishly smiling cat face with a mouth wide open. You may want to create a personalized gift for someone special—a birdhouse in the shape of a boat for a friend who sails, for example, or a gingerbready Victorian birdhouse for an elderly aunt with a penchant for doilies and tea cozies. The possibilities are endless, and the level of craft can be quite impressive.

In the hands of professional craftspeople and artisans, the humble birdhouse can turn into an incredible art piece for inside and outside the home. These artists find a solid market for their creations—birdhouses of all shapes, sizes, and personalities turn up everywhere from knick-knack shops to low- and high-end nurseries to chic interior-design studios. Birdhouses are big business these days, and nowhere are they more prominent than on the Internet, where a search for "birdhouse" turns up hundreds of sites and thousands of birdhouses for sale by artists.

Whether a bird would actually live in some of these houses is doubtful, but form takes precedence over function for these artists. Other home hobbyists and professionals prefer to build birdhouses that are 100 percent functional. Different birds have different housing needs, as detailed in the chart on pages 126–127. These purists build their birdhouses to satisfy every requirement in order to attract a particular species to an acceptable habitat.

There is a happy middle ground. The projects in this book are whimsical in form yet designed to be fully functional as habitats. If you follow the few parameters, such as the size of the entry and interior dimensions, for example, your creation will provide a much-needed nesting spot for the birds in your neighborhood—and a delightful sculptural addition to your garden as well.

Whatever your goal, you should feel free—and, indeed, encouraged—to use these patterns as a template for your ideas. So jump right in—you'll soon find that building a birdhouse is about the most fun you've had in the workshop since that long ago rainy Saturday afternoon.

ABOVE: Home-crafted birdhouses make wonderful personalized gifts. What train aficionado could resist a birdhouse fashioned as a replica of a jaunty caboose, sitting on a section of track for its base?

RIGHT: Imagination—as well as a comic sensibility—knows no bounds when it comes to birdhouse design, as evidenced by this ultra-literal take on the traditional form: a house that looks like a bird.

LEFT: One way of enticing a feathered friend to nest is to provide room and board. A nearby water source can close the sale, as long as it is kept fresh and the dish out of reach of the local calculating cat.

BELOW: Employing the full-service approach, this clever design couples a birdhouse "barn" with an automatic feed dispenser and nectar font "silo."

BOTTOM: Birds of a feather flocking together in a "village" of rustic birdhouses is a visual treat, especially when they are rendered with quaint found materials such as sticks, old weathered fence boards, and even a discarded license plate for a roof.

The Basic Birdhouse

Of the 650 species of birds that make North America their home, you may be surprised to learn that only 85 seek enclosures to build their nests and raise their young. These are known as cavity nesters, and normally they seek out tree and log hollows, eaves, and other sheltered areas—anywhere they can tuck their nests out of direct exposure to the elements and away from predators.

Not surprisingly, natural nesting sites for cavity nesters are decreasing precipitously as mature trees and woods make way for suburban tracts. If building a functional birdhouse is your interest, you can rightly take pride in the fact that you are filling a real need in supporting and fostering the local bird population.

For a functional birdhouse, less is often more. Unfinished, untreated rough wood suffices for the roof, walls, and floor. Hinging one panel is essential for proper clean-out and general maintenance.

There is great satisfaction in hosting birds in your yard. The sensory pleasures of the sight and sound of birds cheer us all. For children, a functional birdhouse can be a wonderful learning experience as they observe the nesting and birthing cycle and take on the responsibility of properly maintaining the nests. The sense of accomplishment and self-esteem gained from successfully providing a habitat can give them a lifelong appreciation for wildlife and ecosystems.

When building for birds, you will want to keep one thing in mind: birds know nothing about art. Wit and whimsy are lost on them—in fact, a little too much whimsy may send them packing. What most of them want, plain and simple, is an enclosure that gives them what they would otherwise find in nature: natural wood that blends well with its environment; the right size entry hole to allow easy passage but keep out weather and predators; the right amount of interior space; good ventilation and drainage; a solid mounting set at an appropriate distance from the ground (although some, including meadowlarks and many sparrows, prefer ground level); inviting surroundings (woodsy or open, depending on the species); and the right amount of territory free from competitors—think of it as personal space. Before you panic, be assured that all of these requirements have been carefully studied and chronicled by the experts in the field and are standardized. The chart on pages 126–127 provides you with the specifications for the most common species of cavity nesters.

Softwoods, such as white pine, Douglas fir, red and Western red cedar, and redwood, in 1-by thickness, make perfect birdhouse material. They are easy to work, and the cedars and redwood weather particularly well outdoors. Birds prefer a rough rather than smoothly sanded texture to the wood but will not turn up their beaks if all other specifications are met. Absolutely none of the interior wood should be painted, chemically coated, or otherwise sealed since these materials can be toxic to birds.

Ideally, the exterior likewise should be left natural. If your urge to paint cannot be denied, try using matte, or flat finish, paint in earthy tones—keep the high-gloss tomato red for the birdhouse you build for your mantel. Shiny bright paint will scare away just about every species, except for the purple martin, a clannish bird that actually prefers bright white multi-bird condos fashioned from aluminum or even from PVC.

And speaking of metal, while you might be tempted to fashion a rustic roof from corrugated tin, copper, or other metals, be aware that those materials heat up quickly and can rapidly turn your birdhouse into an oven depending on your climate and the birdhouse's location. Use metal sparingly and save the heavy-metal applications for your art pieces. Otherwise, feel free to decorate the exterior with whatever natural, or at minimum, nonthreatening bits and pieces you can find. Moss is an attractive material, as are twigs, acorns, straw, hemp and other natural rope material, pine

cones, other cut-wood shapes such as stars or moons, even small stones and seashells. Or, if you are a purist, simply leave it as is.

The key to the success of your useful birdhouse, however, remains its ability to function. The entry needs to be the right size for the bird you want to attract. It's not simply a matter of them fitting in the front door— it also has to do with whom they want to keep out, such as larger predator birds, rats, and cats. Small birds, for example, want an opening no larger than 2 inches in diameter or they won't enter. And, before you start getting fancy with your scroll saw, keep the entry round. It must be placed at a certain height from the birdhouse floor— generally either mid-wall or between mid-wall and the roof. You will need to drill several small holes near the roof for ventilation (heat rises in a birdhouse the same as in your house). You will also need to drill several holes in the floor for drainage. The roof should be hinged for easy maintenance and locked down with a fastener to prevent a wily cat or raccoon from getting ideas. These features sound elemental, but if they are not done right, birds will give your house the claw's down and move on.

Part of the proper functioning of the birdhouse is its location. The most perfect birdhouse, poorly sited, ends up an unused garden fixture. Some birds like leafy, woodsy surroundings, others prefer open land. Most of them like to have a tall bush nearby, which can serve as a convenient resting spot pre- and post-entry. A helpful, and kind, gesture is to place a cat-secure water source nearby, and perhaps a feeder tray. Also follow the guidelines for the required height from the ground to the entry hole.

If you do your job properly—and it isn't hard to do—you will be rewarded with a fine feathered family in the near future, and, with luck and good maintenance, generations of happy, healthy birds that call your yard home.

ABOVE: Birdhouses don't need to be elaborate to exude charm. This stark grouping of single and double birdhouses fashioned from aged Pennsylvania barn siding, for example, evokes a Shaker simplicity that recalls a bygone age. Colony clusters such as this appeal to starlings, which nest in groups.

BELOW: The size of the entry hole is critical to attracting birds. Most small cavity nesters demand an entry hole 2 inches in diameter or less, mainly for protection against predators.

Dressing It Up

The birdhouse offers such a wealth of creative possibilities that it is easy to see why woodworkers and craftspeople sometimes can't contain themselves to purely functional specimens. The projects presented here manage to play with the form in intriguing ways yet still respond fully to a bird's needs and desires. If function is not a priority for you—if you are really interested in giving free rein to your imagination as well as your woodworking skills—the sky is the limit. There are so many options, in fact, that it can be difficult to know where to start.

For home hobbyists and fine artists alike, the birdhouse itself is just the beginning, like a canvas awaiting the magic of paint, embellishment, application. Woodworkers can particularly relish the prospects of honing and exploring tools and talent when contemplating building a birdhouse. They make wonderful, unique gifts, touching keepsakes for children and grandchildren, proud creations for your own home. Perhaps best of all, they are great fun to build.

There are so many options, so many directions you can go when planning your project that you may want to make some decisions before starting.

There are three basic approaches to birdhouse building. One is to embellish the traditional birdhouse box structure. For example, turn the simple wood house into a quaint country cottage with real thatch roof and casement windows, or a bell-towered church with colored glass windows, or a drop-dead likeness of the White House. How satisfying would it be to replicate your own home—or your child's tree house, or a lighthouse you visited during your Maine vacation, or a friend's getaway house on the lake—in birdhouse form? Imitating real-life structures is a good, although not always simple, way to turn the common birdhouse into a personalized keepsake.

ABOVE: With a painted half-moon and a shed door, this outhouse, er, birdhouse gives a nod to a more rustic lifestyle.

LEFT: A clapboard treatment lends textural interest to this otherwise unadorned birdhouse.

ABOVE LEFT: Covered with "graffiti," the basic birdhouse becomes the ultimate urban statement.

ABOVE RIGHT: A simple paint treatment on this traditional birdhouse facade adds panache by mirroring its environment.

RIGHT: Attaching a natural twig wreath to the entry and posting a miniature birdhouse on a pole adds both style and a humorous tweak to the classic birdhouse.

The real effort in such projects as these is not the building of the basic box structure but the level of painstaking detail you choose to take on.

A second approach is to play with the basic box structure. Throw aside the T-square and start to play with shapes. Curve the walls, blow out the roof, cant the entire structure like the leaning tower of Pisa, make the box wriggle like a snake or stand four-square like a chest of drawers. Drill not just one entry hole but a dozen in the facade until the birdhouse resembles a piece of Swiss cheese. Pound enough nails halfway in until it resembles a porcupine. Fashion a round palm frond–topped hut or a steely sky-scraper. You might consider turning your woodworking skills to other materials, using hammer and drill on dried gourds, or a mossy log, or a piece of bamboo, or even an old cowboy boot. Playing with shapes takes a bit more skill with the saw and some careful thought to assembly, but the exercise is remarkably energizing and can result in some eye-popping results.

A third approach is to eliminate the box shape altogether. Now you are

TOP: Having your house replicated in birdhouse form creates an instant, treasured heirloom. The increasing popularity of such custom creations has spurred artisans to transcend simple craft to achieve truly artistic results.

ABOVE: Custom house designs come alive through personalized details—a mounted paddle, flying flag, accurate landscaping—but often, they are built as functional birdhouses with appropriate entry hole size and depth from hole to floor, as well as correctly sized (and unpainted) interior nesting space.

LEFT: Any style house can be duplicated. Custom birdhouse builders study clients' photos, analyzing everything from roof pitch to the smallest architectural details, even requesting roofing and exterior paint samples from the real house to guarantee authenticity.

truly free to work that jigsaw and scroll saw with great abandon. Imagine a birdhouse shaped like a teepee, or a beehive, or your cousin's boat, or your best friend's beloved guitar as a gift for his fiftieth birthday. How about one sporting a tomato-shaped facade, topped with a sassy carved wood tomato bug, for your mother-in-law to place amid her usual bountiful crop? What about a birdhouse shaped like a bird? As long as your creation features a round entry hole, and perhaps an ornamental perch of some sort, you will have built a birdhouse, no matter how outlandish the form.

Materials play a big role in freewheeling birdhouse construction. Since a bird most likely won't be making his or her home there, you can experiment with such materials as metals, stones, plant material, plastic, even glass. You can stucco the exterior and set in stones, or slather it with mastic and cover it in broken tile pieces. You can upholster the wood, or cover it in leather, or feather it. You can indulge your painting whims, break out the neon paint, create a splatter-painted homage to Jackson Pollock, or satisfy your passion for polka dots. Some of the best and most interesting sources of embellishment come from Mother Nature herself. Pieces of driftwood, seed pods, dried flowers, particularly sunflowers, and dried ornamental fruit such as pomegranates, all types of nuts and seeds, as well as seashells or smooth sea glass are all terrific decorative elements for birdhouses—and cheap, too. For the woodworker, birdhouse building can become addictive. All it takes is a few tools, some woodworking basics, and a dash of imagination.

ABOVE: Let Mother Nature do the work of dressing up your birdhouse. Here, lush flowers and foliage adorn a simple multi-family birdhouse.

BELOW: This mantel tableau of three graphically painted chests of drawers becomes a stylish conversation starter when some fowl friends come to roost. Did those sassy birds drill their own entry hole into one?

The Business of Birdhouses

Birdhouses are becoming big business. While they have not yet reached official collectible status the way birdcages have, for example, the market for artisanal and fine-art birdhouses is undeniably there, and growing. Prices in the high-end art market can reach $1,500 and more for luxe materials, such as fine ceramic, glass, or even crystal; limited-edition designs; and one-of-a-kind pieces such as a replica of your home.

As you've probably observed, birdhouses of all types and quality can be found just about everywhere, from gift shops to garden-supply warehouses. If you're shopping for finer specimens—collectibles—you will want to search out artisan stands at county and state fairs, street art fairs, fine garden shops including gift shops at public gardens and arboretums, local galleries, department stores, interior design shops, antiques shops, galleries, and garden

ABOVE: An inventive combination of simple woodworking and paint treatments with found materials—a gilt frame and twig perch—make a birdhouse suitable for, well, framing.

RIGHT: Playing with birdhouse architecture is one of the most fun and satisfying pursuits of the imaginative woodworker. These fantastic handcrafted structures are fashioned from wood culled from a 77-year-old schoolhouse purchased by the artist, who uses its tongue-in-groove lumber and door panels for birdhouse ceilings and walls and old tin for the roofs.

design catalogs. Several local chapters of the American Institute of Architects sponsor annual auctions of one-of-a-kind member-designed birdhouses to benefit the home-building charity Habitat for Humanity. Often, if you see a birdhouse design you like, you can contact the artist or artisan directly.

Undoubtedly, the greatest selection of birdhouses for sale is available on the Internet, although it does take a bit of work to separate the wheat from the chaff. The pursuit is half the fun, however, and, for the craftsperson, can be a great source of inspiration. From the downright schlocky to the sublime, birdhouses can be found at hundreds of sites. The auction site eBay is particularly fertile ground. In one month, nearly 600 birdhouses were offered for auction—everything from traditional log-cabin styles to a Victorian brothel to one resembling Mickey Mouse, in such materials as copper, Swarovski crystal, and old barn wood.

For the serious craftsperson-artist who would like to sell some of his or her wares, the Internet offers an easy marketplace and instant client base. Scanning auction sites can give you an idea of the prices the market will bear, and you can try your hand at offering your designs at auction. If you are really serious, you might try launching your own website, but you will need to be prepared to fulfill multiple orders. Local folk-art and craft shops and street fairs are other venues if you would like to sell your creations in a more personal setting.

Whatever your ultimate goal, birdhouse building is one of life's great pleasures, to enjoy alone or with the companionship of spouse, children, grandchildren, or friends. We hope this book serves as a helpful and continuing inspiration to you to pull out the tools and set your imagination free.

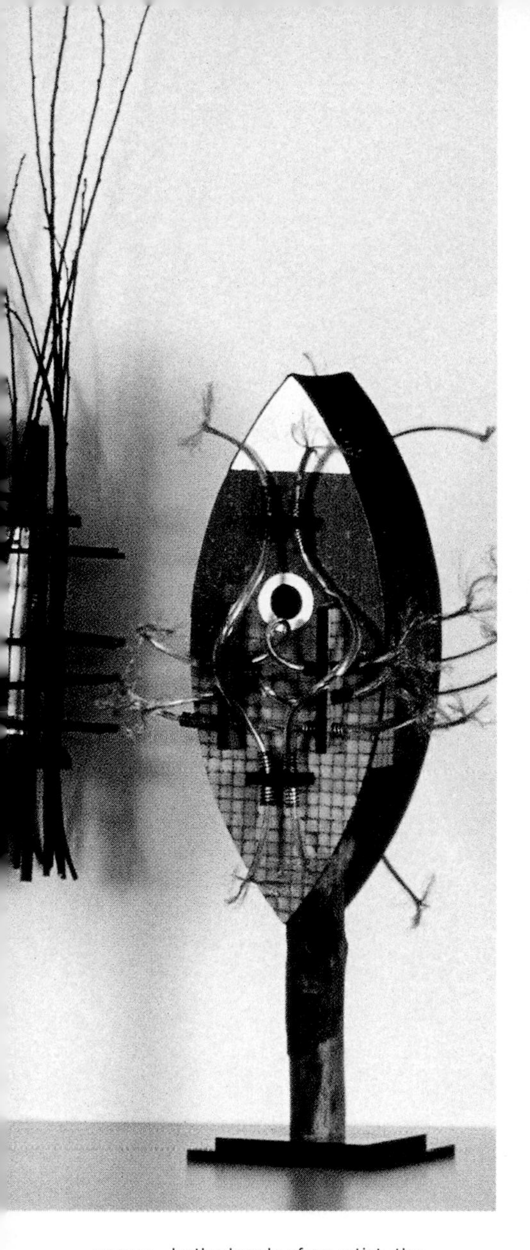

ABOVE: In the hands of an artist, the birdhouse is transformed and transported to fine-art status. Unusual gallery pieces such as these feature the signature entry hole even as they boldly take the traditional birdhouse into new shapes and sculptural forms.

ABOVE RIGHT: Birdhouse art pieces can provide decorating focal points. This sweetly detailed shed-style house, with its dangling teacup, sets the perfect mood for a tea table.

RIGHT: The basic birdhouse becomes a bright sculpture when covered with a mosaic of recycled broken ceramic tiles.

Scientific Nest Box

While this simple nest box may seem like the tract home of birdhouses, it is sturdy; readily attracts an array of species, including Eastern bluebirds, chickadees, house finches, flycatchers, house sparrows, titmice, and more; and, as shown on pages 24–27, can achieve considerable "curb appeal" with a little imagination.

The house is made of ¾-inch lumber, mostly crosscut from standard lumber sizes, so construction is very easy. In fact, it's almost as simple to produce a half dozen or more at a time—and house a whole neighborhood of birds. The solid wood provides good insulation against temperature variations, and vents at the top admit fresh air, or are easily stuffed with weather-stripping putty during cold spells. The swing-out door makes seasonal cleaning easy; it also features a "security panel"—an extra piece that makes the entry hole deeper to foil the reach of cats or other potential marauders. Saw-cuts on the inside of the door provide a ladder for fledglings when it's time for them to try their wings.

The dimensions shown here are based on a 4-by-4-inch floor and 11-inch inside height. To create a nest box for larger birds, check the chart on pages 126–127 and adjust the size of the pieces as needed.

MATERIALS

- 1-by-6 pine or other softwood: 5 feet
- 1-by-8 pine or other softwood: 1 foot
- 1½-inch outdoor screws
- 3d galvanized nails

OPTIONAL: Exterior wood glue or silicone sealant, fine sandpaper, paint or clear polyurethane finish

TOOLS

- Basic hand tools
- Electric drill, bits, and spade bit or hole saw for entry hole

OPTIONAL: Table saw, jigsaw, electric sander, paintbrushes

PREPARE THE PARTS

Cut all the pieces to the specifications shown in the illustration on page 23.

Position the security panel on the door, setting the opening diameter and height according to the sizing chart on pages 126–127. Nail the door to the security panel.

With a drill and spade bit, bore the entry hole through both pieces at once, as shown below.

Using a rasp or a table saw, bevel the rear edge of the roof to match the angle where the sides meet the back.

With a coping saw or a jigsaw, cut arcs at the top of each side piece. ➤

Bore the entry hole through the security panel and door at the same time.

Attach one side to the backing board, then the floor, the other side, and the roof.

Attach the door with two screws driven about 1¾ inches down from the top.

FINISH & MOUNT

Drill four ⅜-inch drainage holes in the floor, as shown below.

Leave the box unfinished, or sand lightly and coat with a light-colored exterior paint or clear finish. Do not finish the inside (this would make it hazardous to birds).

To mount the box, drive a screw through the top and bottom "tabs" in the backing board. For best protection from varmints, attach the box to a solid fence or mount it on a post or pole.

ASSEMBLE THE BOX

Note the positions of the pieces and the fastener locations in the illustration on the facing page. Drill pilot holes for the screws, and back up the joints with wood glue or a silicone sealant.

Using outdoor screws as shown above, attach one side to the back board, then attach the floor, the other side, and the roof, in that order.

ADD THE DOOR

Make multiple sawcuts on the inside of the door to create the saw-kerf ladder. Attach the door with two screws positioned about 1¾ inches down from the top of the door, as shown at top right; make sure that the door can pivot open without hitting the roof.

Drill a hole at the bottom and insert a nail as a "door lock."

Drill four ⅜-inch holes in the floor to provide for adequate drainage.

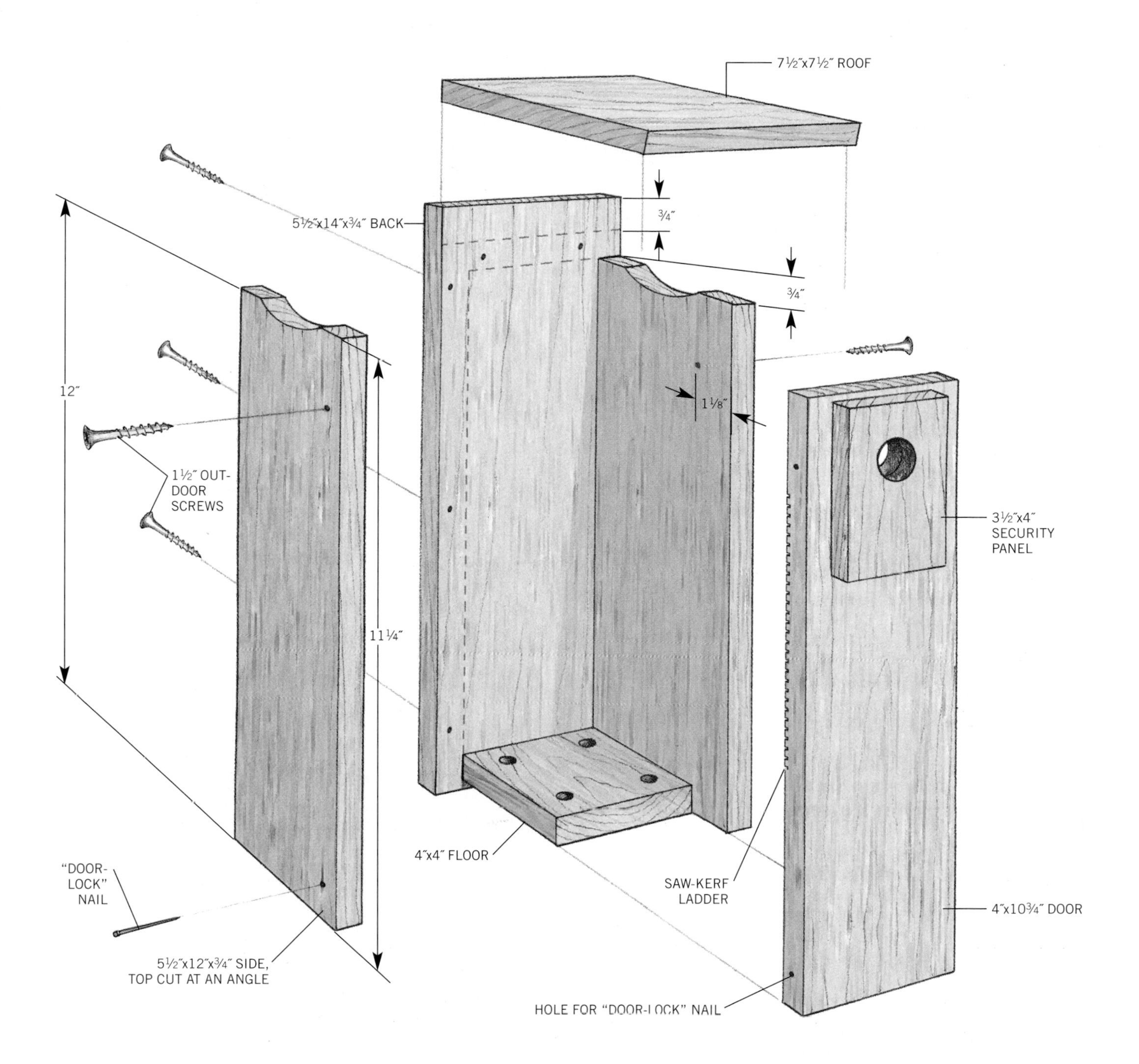
7½″x7½″ ROOF
5½″x14″x¾″ BACK
¾″
¾″
1⅛″
12″
11¼″
1½″ OUT-
DOOR
SCREWS
3½″x4″
SECURITY
PANEL
4″x4″ FLOOR
SAW-KERF
LADDER
4″x10¾″ DOOR
"DOOR-
LOCK"
NAIL
5½″x12″x¾″ SIDE,
TOP CUT AT AN ANGLE
HOLE FOR "DOOR-LOCK" NAIL

Science Dresses Up

While the "scientific" birdhouse on page 20 is the result of considerable research, as an example of architectural style, you could say it's...well...strictly for the birds.

On the inside, this rustic abode is almost exactly the same as the scientific model, but outside it's another matter altogether. Rough-sawn wood and a weathered copper roof add instant character, and the whole project takes only a bit more time than the Scientific Nest Box.

You can copy our design if you like (we've included the pattern), or break out a French curve and have at it on your own.

LAY OUT & CUT THE PARTS

Lay out the sides and back, following the patterns shown on page 26, increased by 400 percent—or create your own patterns, making sure the back and sides are wide enough for a 4-by-4-inch floor and door to fit. Follow our pattern for the top of the back; when you add the roof, it will become clear why.

With a jigsaw or coping saw, cut out all the wooden pieces. Cut out the copper rectangle with tin snips, leaving the corners square for now.

ADD CHARACTER

With a coarse wood rasp, chamfer and distress all the "free" edges of the wooden parts, as shown at right. Also chamfer the back and sides where they meet the roof. Don't rough up the sides where they join the back—you need a tight connection there.

Mount a wire-brush wheel in your drill and, as shown at right, use it to bring out the grain of the cut and rasped edges and to match the surface texture of the rough-sawn wood. Leave the copper roof as-is or texture it with the wire wheel (see the Honeysuckle Cottage, on page 36, for instructions; see also the Copper-clad Barrel House, on page 82, for yet another texture). ➤

Chamfer and distress the exposed edges of the wooden parts, using a coarse wood rasp.

Use a wire-brush wheel to bring out the grain and match the rough-sawn wood's texture.

MATERIALS

- 1-by-6 rough-sawn (S3S) cedar or redwood: 4 feet
- 1-by-8 rough-sawn (S3S) cedar or redwood: 16 inches
- Copper flashing: 9 by 12 inches
- 1½-inch outdoor screws
- 3d galvanized nails
- #4-by-¾-inch round-head brass screws: 4
- Exterior wood glue
- Silicone sealant

OPTIONAL: Paint or stain for the wood, green patina finish for the copper

TOOLS

- Basic hand tools
- Jigsaw, coping saw, band saw, or scroll saw
- Electric drill, bits, and spade bit or hole saw for entry hole
- Wire-brush wheel

OPTIONAL: Table saw

ASSEMBLE THE BOX

Position the security panel according to the opening diameter and height requirements in the sizing chart on pages 126–127. Glue the panel to the door, then drive nails from the door into the panel, making sure to leave clear the area you'll be drilling for the entry. With drill and spade bit, bore the entry hole through both pieces.

Using 1½-inch outdoor screws driven through pilot holes, attach one side to the back, as shown in the illustration opposite; then add the floor, the other side, and the door, in that order. Back up the fixed joints with wood glue or silicone sealant.

Drill a hole through one of the sides into the bottom edge of the door. Insert a nail into this hole as a "door lock."

Paint or stain the box, or leave it natural, like the one shown.

ADD THE ROOF

Place the copper roof over the top, centering it side-to-side, and allowing it to overhang the back by a quarter inch or so. Press it down along the sides and curve of the back.

At the midpoint of each hollow, make a mark, as shown at top left. Drill ⅛-inch holes through the copper at these marks, then drill 1/16-inch pilot holes in the wood and fasten the rear edge of the roof with two brass screws.

Seal the roof-to-back seams with silicone sealant.

Mark, drill, and fasten the roof where it touches the front edges of the sides, using two brass screws.

With tin snips, trim off all four corners of the roof, as shown at top right. Leave the roof to weather on its own, or speed things up with a dose of green patina finish.

Mount this birdhouse in the shade because, in the sun, the metal roof might make the interior too warm for birds to inhabit.

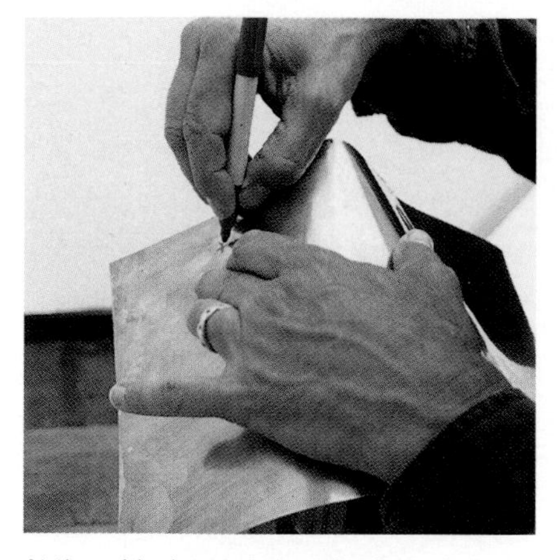

At the midpoint of each roof hollow, mark the location of the brass screws.

Using a pair of tin snips, trim and round off all four corners of the roof.

BACK PATTERN (HALF)

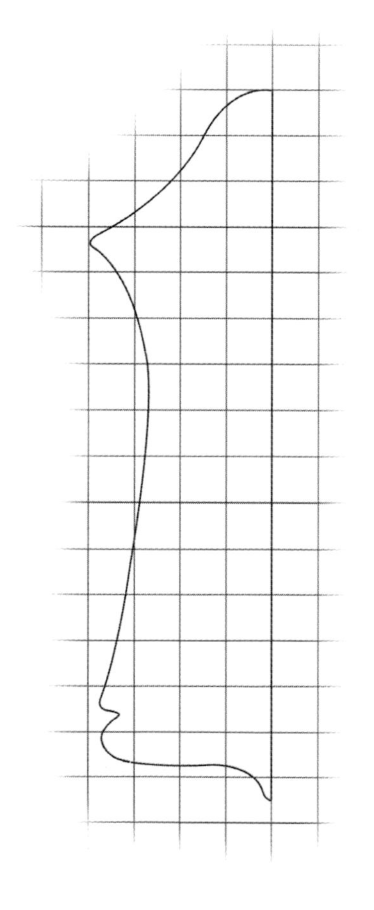

SIDE PATTERN

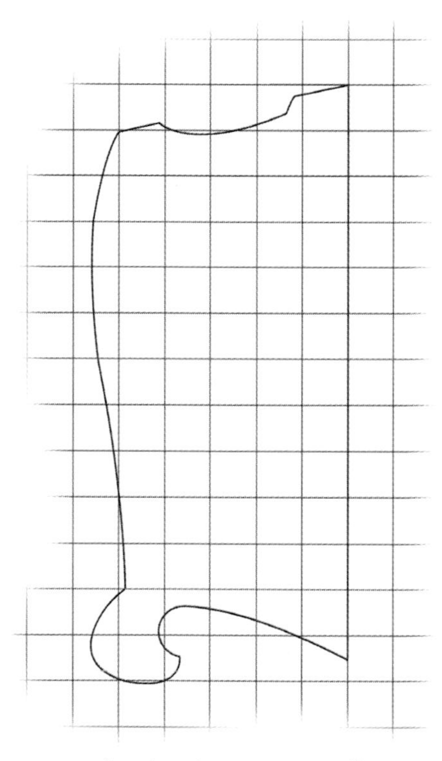

Scale: 1 square = 1″

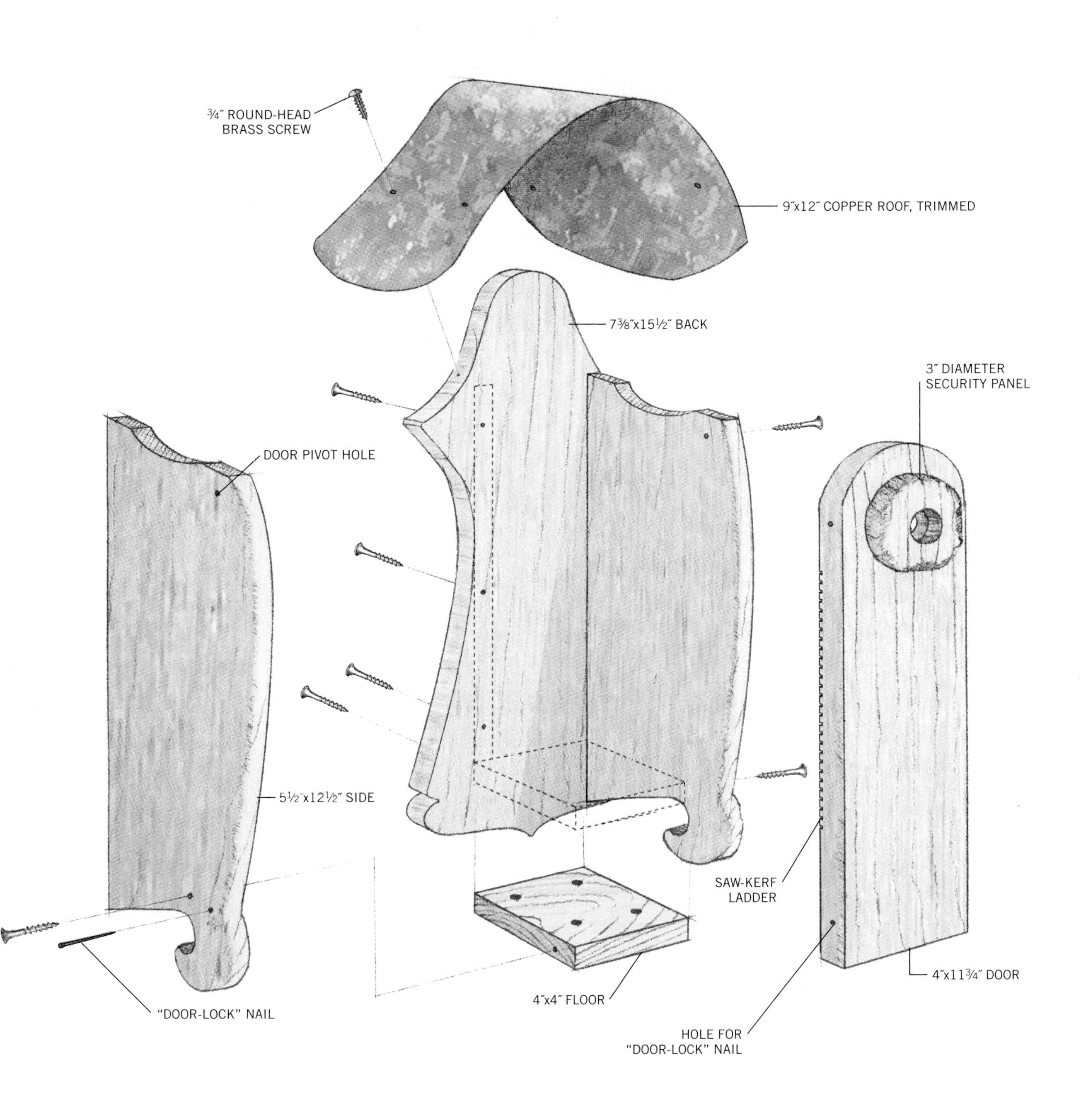

¾″ ROUND-HEAD BRASS SCREW
9″x12″ COPPER ROOF, TRIMMED
7⅜″x15½″ BACK
3″ DIAMETER SECURITY PANEL
DOOR PIVOT HOLE
5½″x12½″ SIDE
SAW-KERF LADDER
4″x11¾″ DOOR
4″x4″ FLOOR
"DOOR-LOCK" NAIL
HOLE FOR "DOOR-LOCK" NAIL

Straw Hut

This whimsical, evocative "hut" is super simple to make—and equally at home as an exotic abode for birds or in a birdhouse collection. As shown on the facing page, an unlikely combination of hardware- and crafts-store items makes for quite a professional-looking result. Best of all, assembly takes only a few minutes.

The hut's core is a length of plastic pipe capped with a plastic funnel. The two huts shown here are clad with twig and grass placemats found at an import store, but anything goes—from a piece of old bamboo roller shade or matchstick blind to bright, patterned fabric or tapa cloth.

The hut is sized for chickadees and other birds that require a 4-by-4 floor (see the chart on pages 126–127), but you can use larger pipe to attract different species. Although not designed for severe weather, the hut's polyurethane coating and waterproof roof make it practical during breeding season. ➤

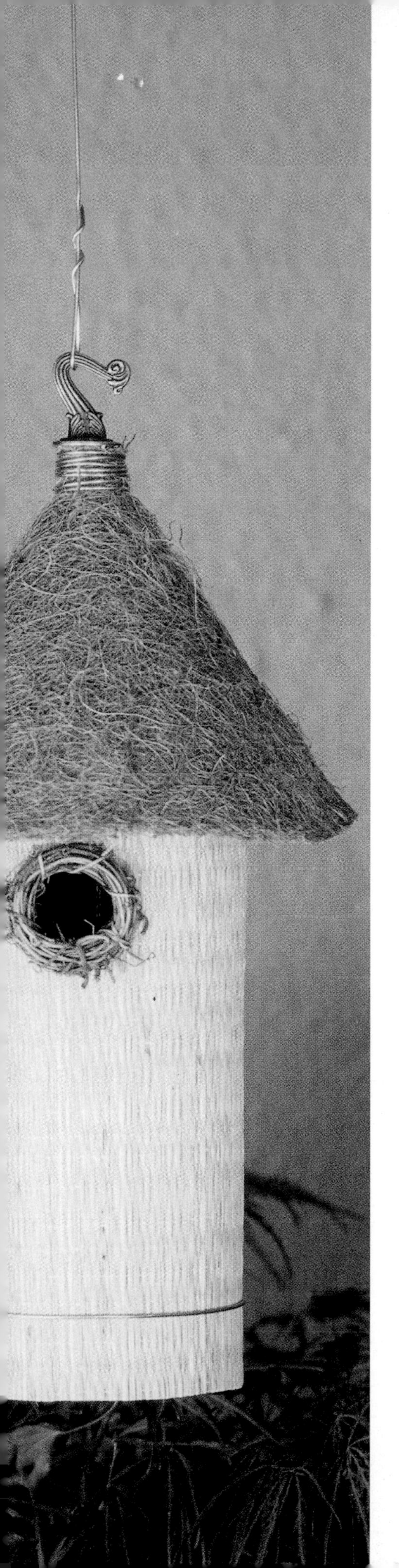

MATERIALS

- 4-inch (inside diameter) ABS or PVC plastic pipe: 1 foot
- Plastic funnel, large enough to cover the pipe (this one was sold as a "transmission funnel" at a hardware store)
- ¾-inch softwood or plywood: 4 inches square
- Straw, grass, or twig placemat: 16 inches long by 8 to 12 inches wide
- Cocoa-mat basket liner: 12 by 12 inches
- Small dried wreath with a 1¾-inch opening (check crafts stores, or make your own from sisal, sea grass, or twigs bound with wire)
- 16-gauge copper wire
- Swag hook and toggle-bolt set
- #6-by-1-inch brass screws: 3
- Hot-melt glue
- Spray polyurethane exterior finish: clear matte or satin

TOOLS

- Basic hand tools
- Hot-melt glue gun
- Electric drill, bits, and spade bit or hole saw for entry hole

OPTIONAL: Jigsaw

These readily available items create a hut that is long on charm and short on expense.

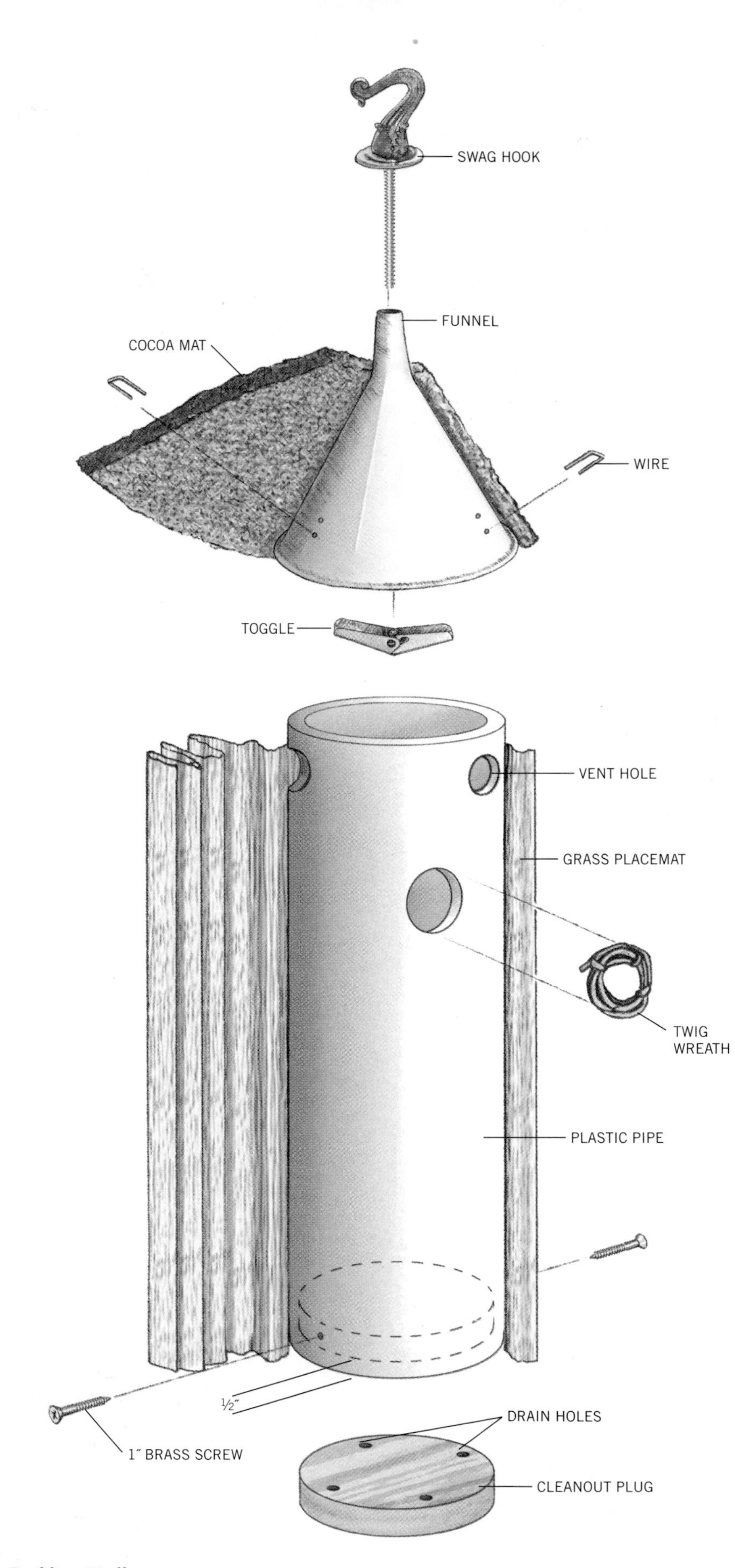

PREPARE THE PARTS

With a crosscut saw, cut the pipe so that it is about ¾ inch longer than the width of the placemat.

With scissors, cut the cocoa mat into a circle 1 foot in diameter, then cut away a quarter of the circle, leaving a three-quarter circle.

Trace the inside diameter of the pipe onto the wood square, and with a coping saw or a jigsaw, cut it to fit snugly inside the pipe.

Drill four ⅜-inch holes in the wood to provide drainage.

DRILL THE HOLES

Drill the entry hole at the height specified in the chart on pages 126–127.

If the hut will be used outdoors, drill two to four vent holes around the upper edge of the pipe, as shown at top left on the facing page.

Clean up the hole edges with a rattail (round) file or sandpaper.

CLAD THE WALLS

Run three or four lines of hot-melt glue around the pipe, as shown at top center on the facing page. Then, starting at the back, opposite the entry hole, wrap the placemat around the pipe, keeping the lower edge of the mat flush with the lower edge of the pipe. The mat will overlap in the back.

When the glue sets, trim off the overlap with a razor knife and glue down the edge. To reinforce the glue, wrap copper wire around the mat about an inch from the top and an inch from the bottom, and twist it together tightly in back with pliers. (This step can be omitted if the hut will not be used outdoors.)

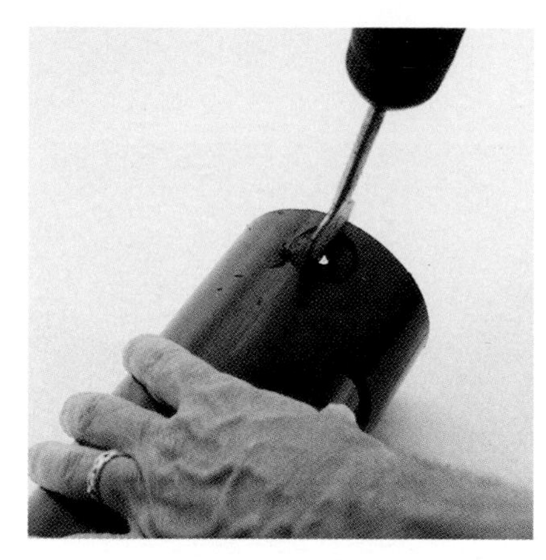

Drill two to four holes around the upper edge of the pipe to allow for ventilation.

After applying three or four lines of hot-melt glue around the pipe, attach the placemat.

Attach the funnel with 3-inch lengths of copper wire bent into the shape of a staple.

ATTACH THE ROOF & FLOOR

With a razor knife, cut away the matting over the entry hole, but leave it in place over the vent holes.

If the hut will not be used outdoors, attach the funnel to the pipe with hot-melt glue, making sure the funnel is perpendicular to the pipe. If the hut will be used outdoors, cut away the matting over the vent holes and wire the funnel in place.

Drill three pairs of ⅛-inch holes spaced equally around the funnel's perimeter. The upper hole of each pair goes through the funnel only; the lower hole goes through the funnel and the pipe (see illustration opposite). Insert 3-inch lengths of copper wire, bent into the "staple" shape shown above right. Reach into the pipe and bend the wire ends upward to secure them in place.

To mount the floor, drill three 3⁄16-inch holes equally spaced around the pipe, about ¾ inch up from the bottom. Attach the floor with three brass screws driven through the holes into the wood. The bottom of the floor will be about a half inch up from the bottom of the pipe.

TRIM & FINISH

Trim off any tabs attached to the funnel's edge so it is smooth.

Apply hot-melt glue liberally to the funnel. Form the cocoa mat into a cone and attach it so the seam is at the back and the funnel's tip protrudes a quarter inch or so from the top. (You might want to give this a dry run before you apply the glue.) The mat will overlap at the back.

When the glue sets, trim away the overlap and glue down the edge. Then trim the perimeter into a neat circle.

Wrap copper wire around the cocoa mat at the base of the funnel's neck, as shown below, and twist it tightly in back with pliers. Then, with a razor knife, trim away the top of the funnel and cocoa mat that sticks up above the copper wire.

Hot-glue the wreath over the entry hole. Assemble the swag hook, push it down into the funnel, and tighten it in place, as shown below.

If the hut will go outdoors, finish the walls and wreath with several coats of exterior polyurethane.

Hang the finished hut from its swag hook, or mount it on a pole, driving a screw through a pilot hole in the back at entry-hole level.

If you plan to hang the finished hut, insert a swag hook into the top of the funnel and tighten.

Cozy Cabin

This simple house uses a classic shape to good advantage. Its broad overhangs and slanted sides reduce the effects of the sun. Ample ventilation slots ensure good air circulation and drainage. The dimensions will accommodate a wide variety of birds (see the chart on pages 126–127), and it's simple to modify them to fit others.

We've jazzed up the house with a unique "sunburst" finish that looks terrific in a garden. Done with leather dyes, it's easy to achieve and fairly glows in the sunshine. Lots of other finishes are possible, too, or you can add "accessories" to suit your whim. The same house appears at the upper right on the cover, with a chimney made from a piece of 1 by 2 and a simple paint job. We've added perches to both houses, but these are recommended only if the house will be used for decorative purposes.

MATERIALS

- 1-by-8 pine or other softwood: 2 feet
- ¼-inch plywood: 2 square feet
- 3d galvanized finishing nails
- 1-inch galvanized hinges with screws: 2
- Small gate hook and eye
- Exterior wood glue
- Fine sandpaper
- Yellow and red leather dyes
- Oil-based wood stain: mahogany red
- Marine varnish

OPTIONAL: 1 by 2 and 1¼-inch drywall screw for chimney, 2-inch-long by ¼-inch dowel for perch, other stain or paint

TOOLS

- Basic hand tools
- Electric drill, bits, and spade bit or hole saw for entry hole

OPTIONAL: Electric sander or grinder, jigsaw, coping saw, band saw, or scroll saw

LAY OUT & CUT THE PARTS

After laying out the parts, cut one end A, then use it as a pattern to draw and cut the other end A. Do the same for sides D. Cut floor B and roof pieces C and E.

Draw a vertical centerline on the inside of ends A. Choosing the one with the most interesting grain, draw a line on the inside connecting the gable corners. Drill the entry hole at the intersection of these lines, boring part way through from the back and finishing from the front.

Sand all the parts and ease any sharp edges.

ASSEMBLE THE BOX

Draw a centerline from front to back on floor B, then match it up with the centerlines on ends A. Glue and nail ends A to floor B, noting that the floor will fall short of the sides to create space for ventilation and drainage.

Glue and nail roof C in place as shown at right, aligning its top edge with the gable peaks and allowing an overhang of 1½ inches at the front and back.

Finally, to allow for ventilation, glue and nail one side D to ends A, positioning it down about ⅛ inch from the underside of the roof and allowing an overhang of ½ inch at each end A.

If you're using the optional chimney, glue and screw it in place, driving the drywall screw from beneath. ➤

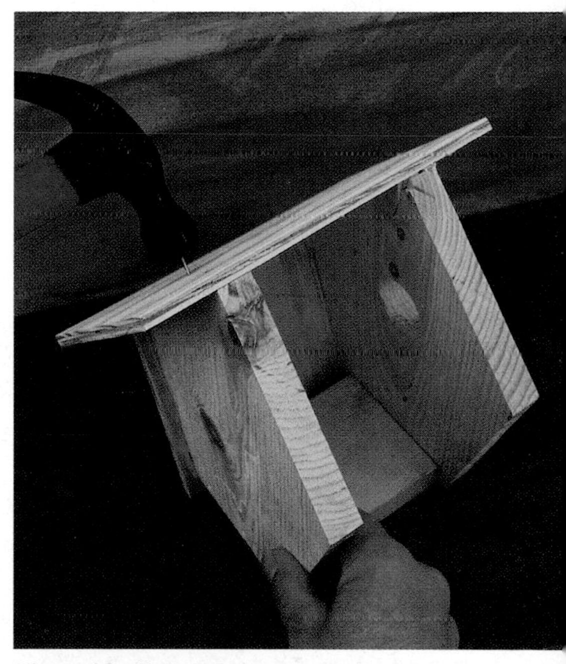

Align roof C with the gable peaks, allowing a 1½-inch overhang, then glue and nail.

Screw the hinges to the roof with their barrels about 2 inches from the gable ends.

Using the applicator that comes with it, apply a flood coat of red leather dye to the roof.

Blend the red dye into the yellow to create a graduated "sunburst" effect.

COMPLETE THE HOUSE

Hold roof E in position, then slide the remaining side D up against it. Trace along side D to mark a line on the underside of roof E where the two pieces meet. Place the hinge barrels flush with the line, about 2 inches in from the gable ends, and screw the hinges to the underside of roof E in the eaves space, as shown above. (The mounting screws will protrude through the top of the roof, but don't worry.)

Holding roof E and side D in place, slide D down from the roof to match the ventilation space on the other side. Mark the screw hole locations onto side D and attach the hinges.

File or grind the protruding screw tips flush with the wood, then glue and nail E in place.

Finally, secure the bottom edge of the hinged side to the floor with the small gate hook.

At this point, you can sand and paint the house, as we did the one on the cover, or proceed to the glowing sunburst finish described in the next two steps.

LAY THE PAINT FOUNDATION

Wipe the roof roughly with a rag barely dampened in the red mahogany stain. Don't try to cover the surface, just apply a little texture that will underlie and add character to the final color. Allow to dry for a few minutes.

Next, using the applicator that comes with leather dyes, apply a flood coat of red dye to the roof surface and edges, as shown above, and a flood coat of yellow to the ends and sides of the house. (Make sure to protect your work surface and wear disposable latex gloves.)

MAKE THE SUNBURST

Working on one side or end at a time, apply a second flood coat of yellow, then immediately follow with a single swab of red around the edges of the panel. Using the yellow applicator, well charged with yellow dye, immediately blend the red into the yellow to create a graduated, "sunburst" effect, as shown above right. (You might want to practice on some scrap—or the backside of the house—before committing to the more visible panels.)

Finally, add red dye under the eaves and gables, and a final coat to the roof. Let dry for a few minutes, and, if you wish, add extra touches of mahogany stain to darken the plywood edges, perimeter of the roof surface, and panel edges. Allow to dry overnight, drill for and add a perch if you like, then finish with two or three coats of marine varnish to make the sunburst really glow.

MOUNT THE HOUSE

You can mount your cabin to a post by screwing directly through the back wall. To attach the house to the top of a post, cut a piece of ¾-inch plywood a little larger than the post diameter. Attach this to the post, and then screw through the plywood into the floor of the birdhouse.

To hang the cabin, drive brass eye screws into the roof at the peak, directly over the end panels. Twist each end of a wire onto the eye screws.

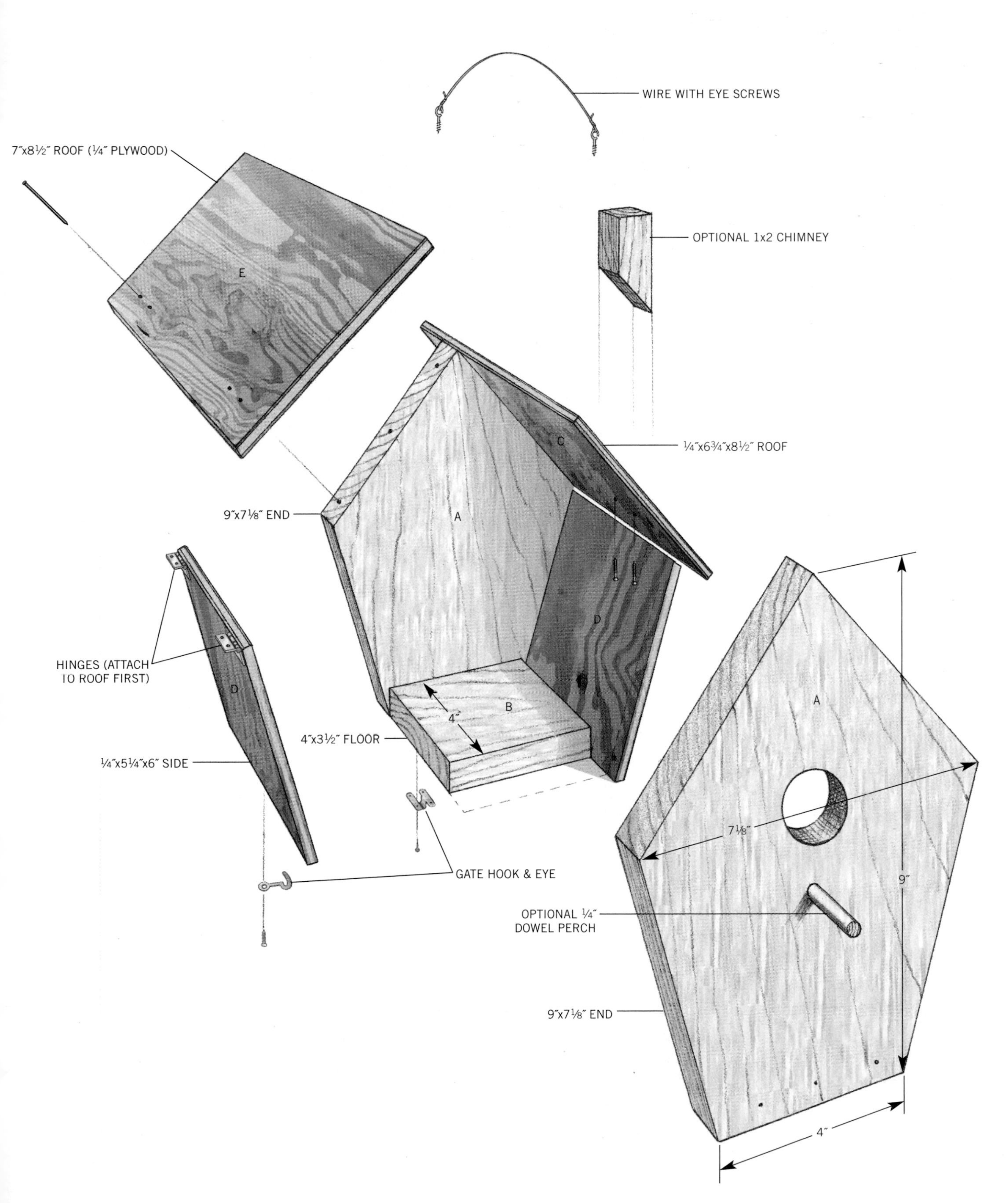

WIRE WITH EYE SCREWS
7″x8½″ ROOF (¼″ PLYWOOD)
E
OPTIONAL 1x2 CHIMNEY
C
¼″x6¾″x8½″ ROOF
9″x7⅛″ END
A
D
HINGES (ATTACH TO ROOF FIRST)
D
4″
B
4″x3½″ FLOOR
¼″x5¼″x6″ SIDE
A
7⅛″
GATE HOOK & EYE
9″
OPTIONAL ¼″ DOWEL PERCH
9″x7⅛″ END
4″

Honeysuckle Cottage

This cozy cottage for feathered friends delivers maximum charm for minimum effort.

You'd never know it from the professional look, but construction is a breeze and stenciling the front is just as easy. The decorative painting is done with tempera paint over a water-based stain so if you make a goof you can just wipe it off and start over. Polyurethane protects your final handiwork.

A ventilated roof and removable floor promote the health of the inhabitants and make cleanout easy.

Cut Out & Prepare the Parts

Enlarge the front and back patterns shown on page 38, trace them onto the 1 by 10, and cut out with a jigsaw or coping saw. Next, cut the sides and bottom from the 1 by 6. The splayed sides require angle cuts where they meet the bottom. For maximum accuracy, make these on a table saw, setting the blade angle to 70 degrees. Or you can use a rasp to make angled flat areas in the bottom where it meets the sides, an option that is nearly as accurate and perfectly functional.

Drill and counterbore the front and rear for screws, as shown in the illustration on page 39.

Cut the copper to size and, if you wish, texture the roof. Fold the copper sheet in half along the ridge line and trim both lower edges at once with tin snips, as shown above right. Hold the copper firmly to your work surface with a scrap of wood, then texture the copper with a wire-wheel brush mounted in a power drill, as shown at top left on page 38. We created the shinglelike texture by making rows of shallow overlapping arcs. Another texture is shown on the bottom of the Copper-clad Barrel House, on page 82.

Make the Stencil & Paint the Front

Enlarge the honeysuckle pattern on page 38 by 400 percent. Mount it to the card stock or file folder with spray adhesive or rubber cement. Cut out the pattern with a razor knife. Paint the stencil with the copper-colored oil-based spray enamel (and while you're at it, paint the wood screw-hole buttons as well).

Wipe all wood parts that will be exposed with water-based wood stain and allow to dry completely. Tape the stencil in place on the front of the ➤

Stenciling the face, adding texture to the roof, and scalloping the roof's edges make this simple birdhouse look like the handicraft of an artisan.

MATERIALS

- 1-by-6 pine or other softwood: 16 inches
- 1-by-10 pine or other softwood: 30 inches
- Copper flashing: 9 by 24 inches
- 1½-inch outdoor screws: 10
- #6-by-¾-inch round-head brass screws: 4
- Brass eye screws: 2
- ¼-inch wood screw-hole buttons: 8
- Exterior wood glue
- Light card stock or a file folder, about 9 by 12 inches
- Spray adhesive or rubber cement
- Fine sandpaper
- Spray enamel: copper color
- Water-based stain: "harvest gold" or similar color
- Tempera paints
- Spray polyurethane exterior finish: clear matte or satin

TOOLS

- Basic hand tools
- Jigsaw, coping saw, band saw, or scroll saw
- Electric drill, bits, and spade bit or hole saw for entry hole

OPTIONAL: Table saw, electric sander

Texture the copper roof with a wire-wheel brush. Hold it firmly with a wood scrap.

Pounce the paint through the openings in the stencil, using a lightly loaded foam brush.

Fasten the roof with brass screws at the deepest part of the roof's curves.

house. With the foam brush, pounce blue and green colors through the stencil openings, as shown at top center. Use only a little paint on the brush.

To get a variegated effect, we used children's tempera paints, pooling colors in plastic dishes and mixing them incompletely in the center. If you let the brush carry several shades at once, you'll get a nice, painterly effect with little effort. When you're done stenciling, paint the centers of the honeysuckle flowers with dots of pure yellow.

Allow the paint to dry, then drill the entry hole. Finish the exposed faces and edges of all wood parts with spray polyurethane (make sure it's oil-based so the paint won't run).

ASSEMBLE THE HOUSE

Attach the rear of the house to the sides with outdoor screws, then add the front. You may glue these connections first if you wish. Glue the painted buttons over the screw holes. Attach the floor with two outdoor screws, as shown in the illustration opposite, but don't glue it: the floor must be removable for seasonal cleaning.

ATTACH THE ROOF & HANG THE HOUSE

Place the roof over the gables until it's seated on the peak and overlaps the front of the house by about an inch. Press it down, then mark and drill 1⁄8-inch holes in the deepest part of the curves on each, front and back (as shown at top right, this will be about two-thirds of the way down either side of the roof). Drill pilot holes in the wood and fasten the roof in place with 3⁄4-inch round-head brass screws.

File notches in the roof peak over the gables with a triangular file. Drill pilot holes, screw the brass eye screws in place, then hang the house from a length of copper wire.

FRONT AND BACK PATTERN, INCLUDING STENCIL LAYOUT

Scale: 1 square = 1″

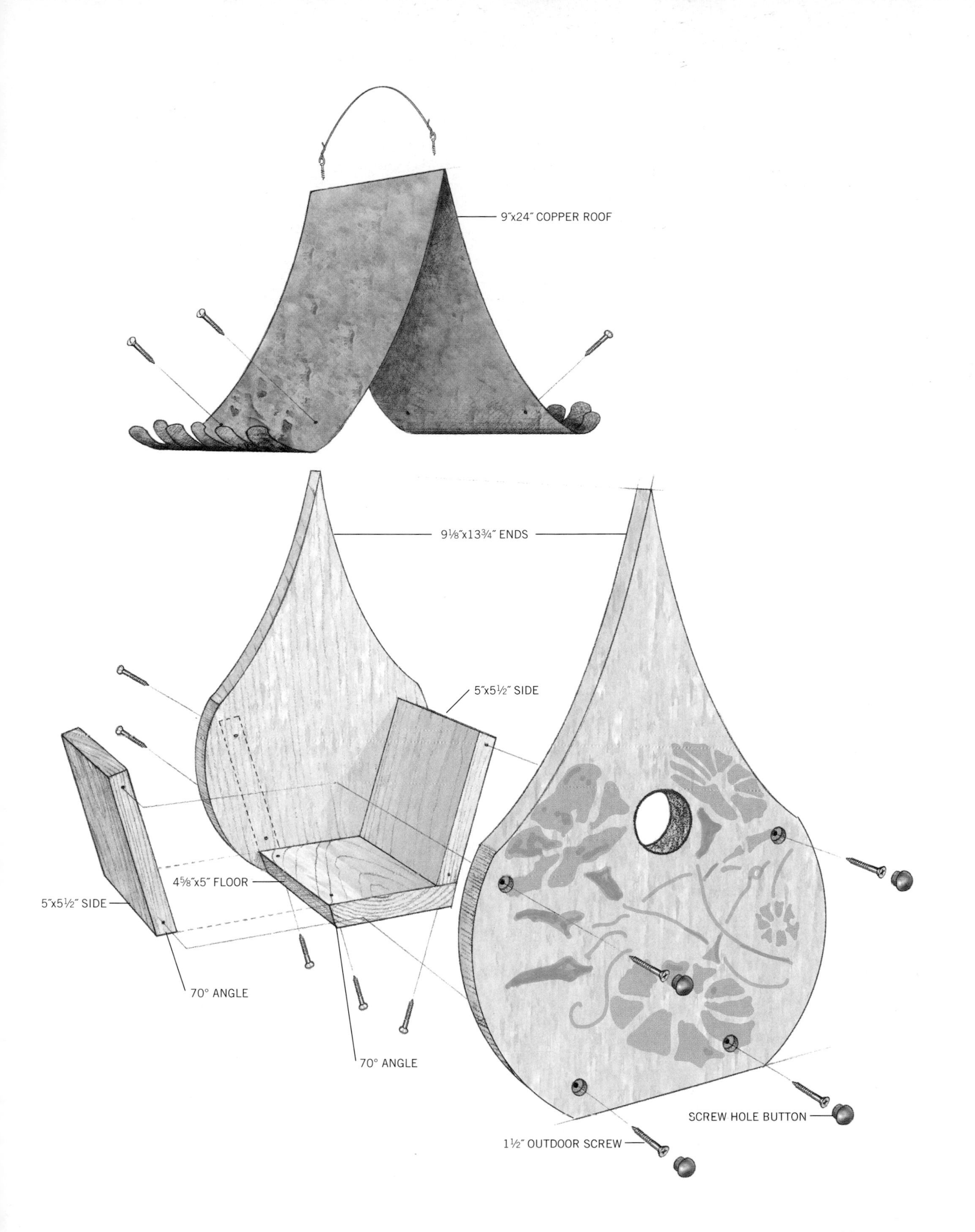
9″x24″ COPPER ROOF
9⅛″x13¾″ ENDS
5″x5½″ SIDE
4⅝″x5″ FLOOR
5″x5½″ SIDE
70° ANGLE
70° ANGLE
SCREW HOLE BUTTON
1½″ OUTDOOR SCREW

Hollow-log Cabin

This woodsy abode is full of character and natural charm. Perhaps best of all, most of the materials are as readily available as a stack of firewood. Construction is quick and easy, and no finishing is required.

Softwoods, such as cedar, redwood, and pine, are easiest to work with, especially if you're using only hand tools. If you have access to a chain saw, then oak, walnut, and other hardwoods are an option. Don't use knotty woods, though, as these won't split cleanly.

The sizes indicated are minimums, and create a 4-inch-square floor. However, construction is so rough-and-ready, you can easily adapt the design to suit the wood you have on hand. Check the sizing chart on pages 126–127 to size the birdhouse for its likely inhabitants.

Dried flowers and raffia twine from a crafts store are optional touches—but help to make this house a home.

MATERIALS

- Straight-grained log, at least 8 inches in diameter by 10 inches
- Straight-grained log, at least 10 inches in diameter by 8 inches
- Tree branch, approximately 1 inch in diameter by 1 foot
- 6d galvanized box nails
- 3-inch outdoor screws
- Steel or copper wire
- Silicone sealant
- Brass eye screws: 2

OPTIONAL: Dried flowers, raffia twine, hot-melt glue

TOOLS

- Basic hand tools
- Chain saw or bow saw
- Heavy wood chisel, brickset, or splitting wedge
- Electric drill, bits, and spade bit or hole saw for entry hole

OPTIONAL: Hot-melt glue gun

PREPARE THE PARTS

With a small chain saw or bow saw, trim one end of the smaller log at a 90-degree angle. Make two 45-degree cuts at the other end to accept the roof panels. Cut the roof panels from the larger log, making sure they will be wide enough to span the house. Note: Be extremely careful if working with a chain saw. Follow all of the saw manufacturer's directions.

Mark a square on the top of the smaller log so that when the sides are split, each will be at least 4 inches at the thickest part. Screw the log to a foot-square scrap of ¾-inch plywood to hold it steady. Then, with a chisel, brickset, or splitting wedge, split the log along the square's lines, as shown at top right. Drill an entry hole in one of the walls.

Next, cut an inch-thick slice from the bottom of the interior waste piece as shown at right; this will become the floor. Drill three or four ⅜-inch drain holes in it.

ASSEMBLE WALLS & FLOOR

Fasten each wall piece to the floor using galvanized nails or outdoor screws (drill pilot holes and counterbore if using screws). A hot-melt glue gun is better than a third hand at this stage; stick the parts together first and they'll hold still for the rest of the operation. Wrap the top with wire and twist the ends tight, as shown at right. The steel wire we used blends in; copper wire will become a design element. ➤

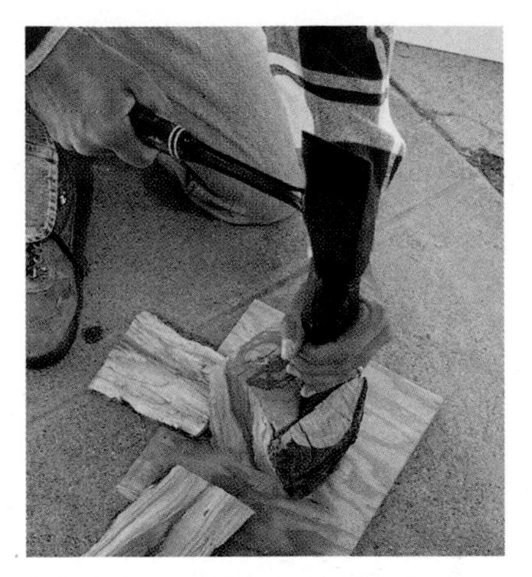

Split the log so that each side piece is at least 4 inches thick at its widest point.

Cut a slice 1 inch thick from the interior waste piece to make the floor of the birdhouse.

Wrap wire tightly around the tops of the sides and twist to hold the pieces firmly together.

To hang the house, add eye screws with wire to the branch atop the roof.

ADD ROOF & TRIM

Trim the roof pieces to fit and attach each piece with two 3-inch outdoor screws. Drill pilot holes and counterbore for the screws. Stuff drill shavings into a drop of glue on top of each screw head to hide the screws. Seal the top seam with silicone sealant.

Bind dried flowers to the tree branch with raffia twine, if you like (we show sturdy wood roses). Attach the tree branch with two counterbored outdoor screws.

HANG THE HOUSE

Add eye screws and wire, as shown at left. Cut 2 feet of wire, double it, and clamp the free ends in a vise. Then chuck a bent nail in an electric drill, hook its head in the wire loop, draw it tight, and pull the trigger to wind the wire.

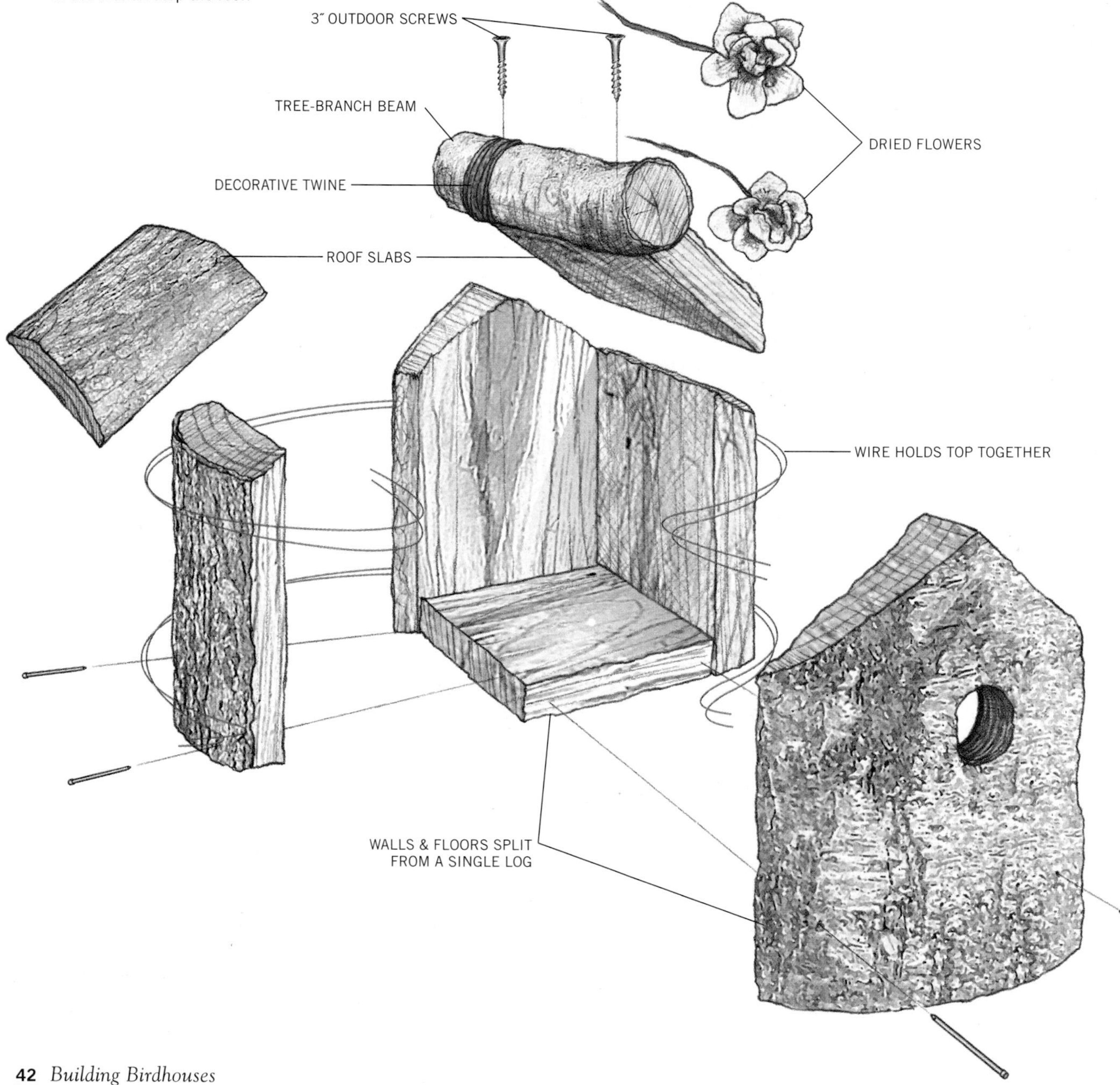

The Basic Birdhouse

Why does a "basic birdhouse" look like an icon of a human house? Probably because this form is familiar to us, its simple roof sheds rain, and it's easy to build. Fortunately, this shape makes a great nesting box for all kinds of birds. Use the dimensions shown on page 45 and the house will accommodate the widest variety of birds, as listed in the sizing chart on pages 126–127.

Above all, this is an easy-to-build "blank canvas" that's simple for even a child to help make. With a table saw to aid cutting, it's very easy to construct a half dozen of these at once. Each can be cut from a single 5-foot 1 by 6.

For additional treatments of this basic house, see the Little Red Schoolhouse, Mock Tudor, Tin Shack, and A Touch of the East on pages 46–58. ➤

MATERIALS

- 1-by-6 pine or other softwood: 5 feet
- 3d galvanized finishing nails
- 1½-inch outdoor screws: 2
- Hot-melt glue or exterior wood glue
- Spackling compound
- Fine sandpaper
- Water- or oil-based paint
- Spray polyurethane exterior finish: clear satin

OPTIONAL: Glitter glue, gold leaf, appliqués, stencils, etc.

TOOLS

- Basic hand tools
- Electric drill, bits, and spade bit or hole saw for entry hole

OPTIONAL: Jigsaw, coping saw, band saw, or scroll saw, electric sander

CUT OUT THE PARTS

Using the chart opposite, cut out all of the pieces. If you're using a handsaw, make the crosscuts first, then make the four rip cuts (pieces B, D, and E). If you're using a power saw, rip all of the 4-inch-wide pieces, then cross cut.

The 90-degree gables are cut at 45 degrees to the edge of the board; a try square makes it easy to mark the cutting lines.

Mark the center of the entrance hole on one piece C, and drill it with a 1⅜-inch spade bit or hole saw. Bevel the back edge of the floor, E, as shown in the illustration opposite.

ASSEMBLE THE BOX

Glue and nail roof piece A to roof piece B and set aside. Connect the sides, D, to the back, C.

Use glue and 3d finishing nails for all connections. Drill 1⁄16-inch pilot holes for the nails so you won't split any pieces. Countersink the nails. (Hot glue makes a great "third hand," holding parts in alignment for nailing.)

Next, position the floor. If it doesn't pivot freely, use a sander or rasp to trim it. Drill ⅛-inch pilot holes and fasten with outdoor screws, as shown at top left. A nail serves as a latch to hold the floor in position: to install it, drill a 3⁄32-inch hole 1 inch deep through the side and into the floor.

Glue and nail the front, C, in place. Position the roof and drill pilot holes to fasten it to the front and rear, but don't install it yet.

Attach the floor with outdoor screws; it is beveled at the back to permit it to pivot freely.

Applying paint to the house without an undercoat will allow the wood grain to show through.

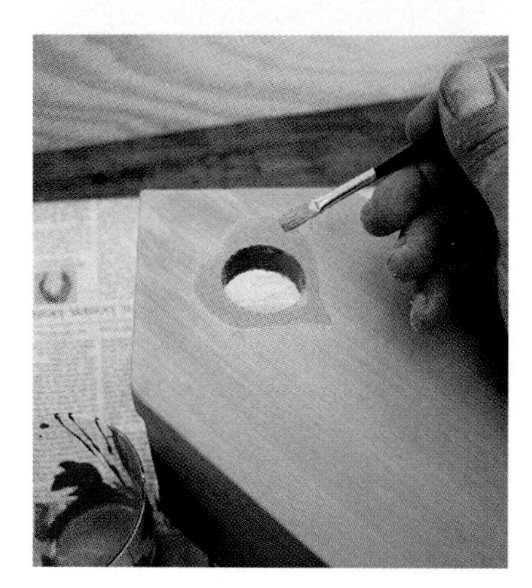

Paint decorative touches onto the front and sides of the birdhouse.

Add any finishing touches to the roof once the house construction is complete.

PREP & PAINT THE HOUSE & ROOF

Fill the nail holes and screw heads with spackling compound, then sand all surfaces smooth, round off all sharp edges, and dust thoroughly.

Apply paint coats to the house and roof, as shown at top right, starting with an undercoat if you don't want to see the wood grain. We used thin, water-based tempera paint to create a semitransparent wash that lets the grain show through. Don't forget to paint under the roof overhang at gables and eaves.

For a folk-art look, wipe the base coat away in places when it's wet. For a distressed look, let the paint dry, then use fine sandpaper to sand through it in places.

ATTACH THE ROOF & ADD DESIGN ELEMENTS

We used oil-based paint for the swoopy heart shape over the entry hole, as shown above left (be sure to paint the interior of the hole). Using oil-based paint ensures that the tempera undercoat remains intact.

Glue and nail the roof in place.

With the house complete, add any other design elements that suit your fancy, such as the flowers we added to the roof eaves, as shown above. When the paint is dry, topcoat the house with spray satin polyurethane.

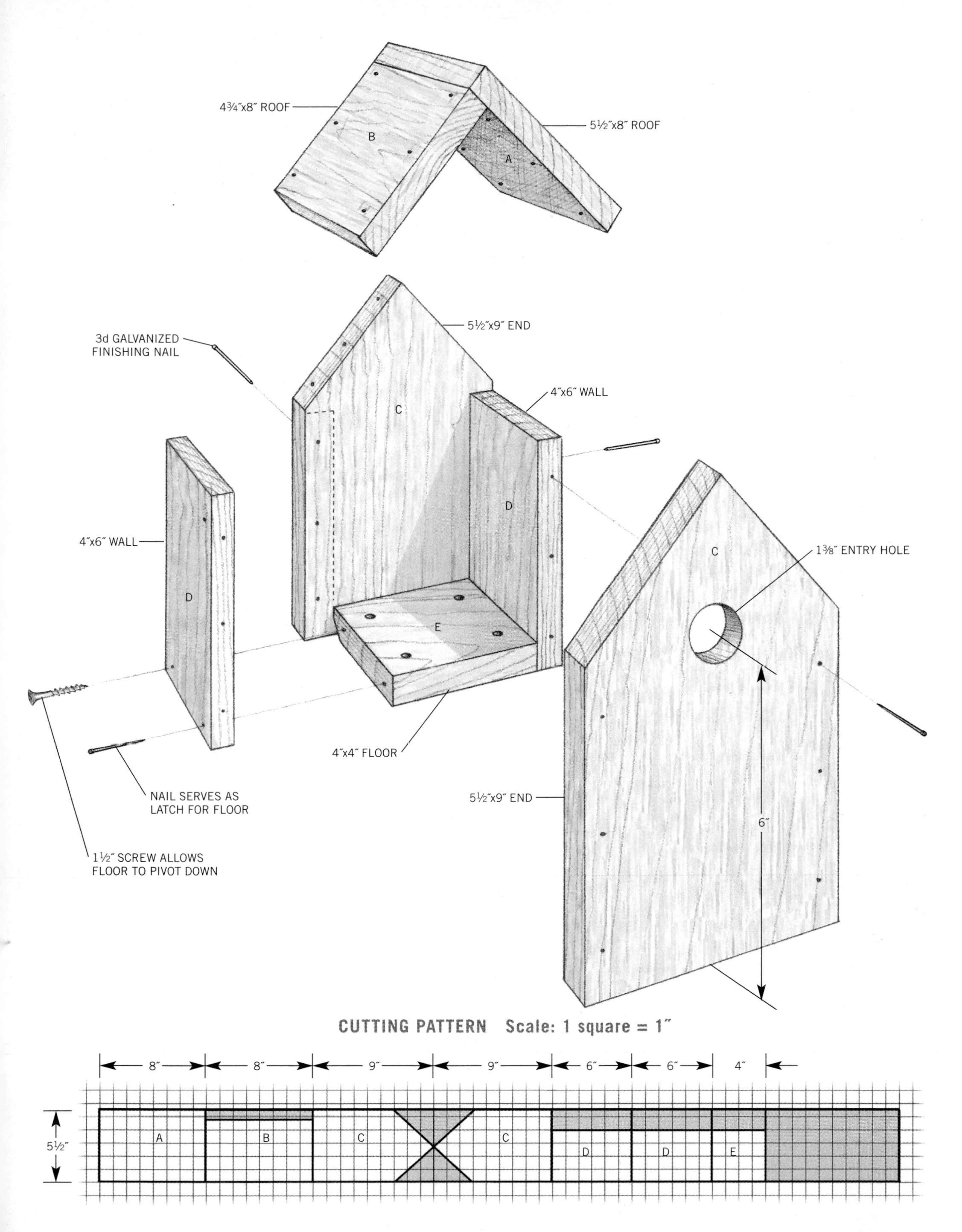
4¾″x8″ ROOF
5½″x8″ ROOF
B
A
5½″x9″ END
3d GALVANIZED FINISHING NAIL
C
4″x6″ WALL
D
4″x6″ WALL
D
E
C
1⅜″ ENTRY HOLE
4″x4″ FLOOR
NAIL SERVES AS LATCH FOR FLOOR
5½″x9″ END
6″
1½″ SCREW ALLOWS FLOOR TO PIVOT DOWN
CUTTING PATTERN Scale: 1 square = 1″
8″
8″
9″
9″
6″
6″
4″
5½″
A
B
C
C
D
D
E

Little Red Schoolhouse

Although this Victorian schoolhouse is the most complicated birdhouse in our Basic Birdhouse series, it's still just a weekend project. It achieves its flair mostly from painted moldings that are easily applied. You can vary the design to suit your whim, too. Although intended primarily for display, the house can be used outside during the nesting season—where the fledglings can attend a little preflight school.

MATERIALS

- Basic Birdhouse (see page 43) without floor
- ¼-inch plywood, 5½ by 8 inches
- 2-by-2 softwood: 4 inches
- ¼-by-¾-inch flat molding: 3 feet
- ⅛-by-¼-inch thin wood trim: 6 feet
- ¼-inch wood dowel: 8 inches
- 3-inch self-adhesive aluminized roof flashing or cedar shims
- ⅝-inch brads
- 3d galvanized finishing nails
- ¾-inch drywall screws: 2
- Hot-melt glue or exterior wood glue
- Fine sandpaper
- Water- or oil-based paint: flat white; red, green, and pale blue enamels
- Spray polyurethane exterior finish: clear satin

OPTIONAL: Red leather dye

TOOLS

- Basic hand tools
- Jigsaw, coping saw, band saw, or scroll saw
- Electric drill, bits, and spade bit or hole saw for entry hole
- Foam brush

OPTIONAL: Table saw, electric sander

PREPARE THE PARTS

First build the Basic Birdhouse, as discussed on pages 43–45. Note in the illustration on page 49 that you must make the floor larger and run it under the back, sides, and front.

Cut, notch, and bevel a 4-inch length of 2 by 2 for the belfry and cut the gingerbread pieces as shown in the illustration on page 49. Rip the thin trim from ¾-inch stock using a table saw, or cut it from the molding with a utility knife and straightedge. Make the steps from the molding.

Paint or stain the birdhouse and belfry red (we used red leather dye, from a hobby supply shop, because it lets the wood grain show through). Paint the floor green. Paint the roof, dowels, and all of the molding and trim white.

If using aluminized roof flashing, roll out about 4 feet and, with a pair of scissors, cut it down the middle into two 1½-inch strips; then crosscut the strips into 8-inch pieces. If you prefer to use cedar shims, cut them into shingle-size pieces. ➤

Start with a Basic Birdhouse and add a belfry, gingerbread trim, aluminum shingles, and a picket fence to make this fun variation anything but basic.

Attach the trim and gingerbread pieces with exterior wood glue if the house will be placed outside; otherwise hot-melt glue will suffice.

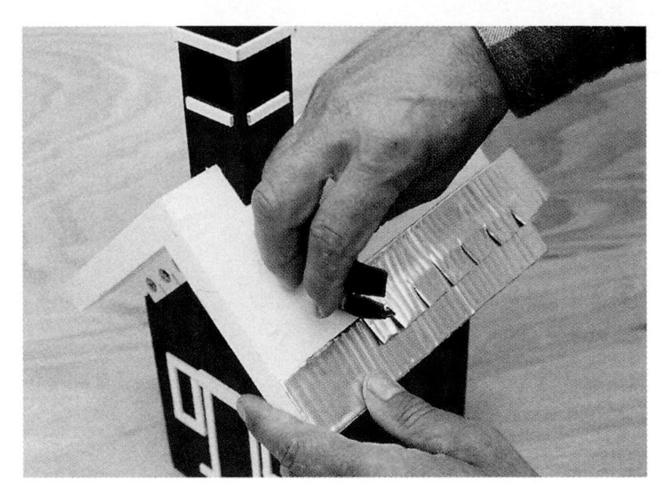
Cover the roof with aluminized flashing strips notched with scissors to simulate slate shingles; they come with self-adhesive backing.

Affix the stairs to complete the project—almost. To finish, touch up the trim and paint the door and windows, then add mullions.

ASSEMBLE THE HOUSE

Glue the thin trim to the belfry, glue and nail the belfry to the roof, then the roof to the house.

On the front of the house, as shown at top left, attach the windows and the door made from the thin trim, as well as the gingerbread pieces, with exterior wood glue if the house will be placed outside and with hot-melt glue if not. Cut the corner pieces from the molding and attach them using glue and small brads since these pieces are the most likely to be knocked off in handling.

ATTACH THE ROOF

Nail the roof in place with 3d finishing nails. Add flashing strips to the roof as shown bottom left, notching them with scissors to simulate slate shingles. Or, install shingles cut from cedar shims instead (see the Seashell Sand Castle on page 78 for instructions on preparing the shims).

ADD A FENCE & STAIRS

Attach the floor, flush at the back, with two drywall screws driven into each side from the bottom. Drill 1/4-inch holes in the front of the floor, glue in the four 2-inch dowel pieces, then glue the cross-rails in place. Finally, as shown above, glue the stairs in place.

Touch up the cut ends of all the trim with white paint. Paint the door white and the windows pale blue. When the blue paint is dry, add white mullions with the pointed tip of a foam brush.

If you'd like to age your schoolhouse, rub the corners and edges with a damp tea bag. When dry, spray on several coats of satin polyurethane.

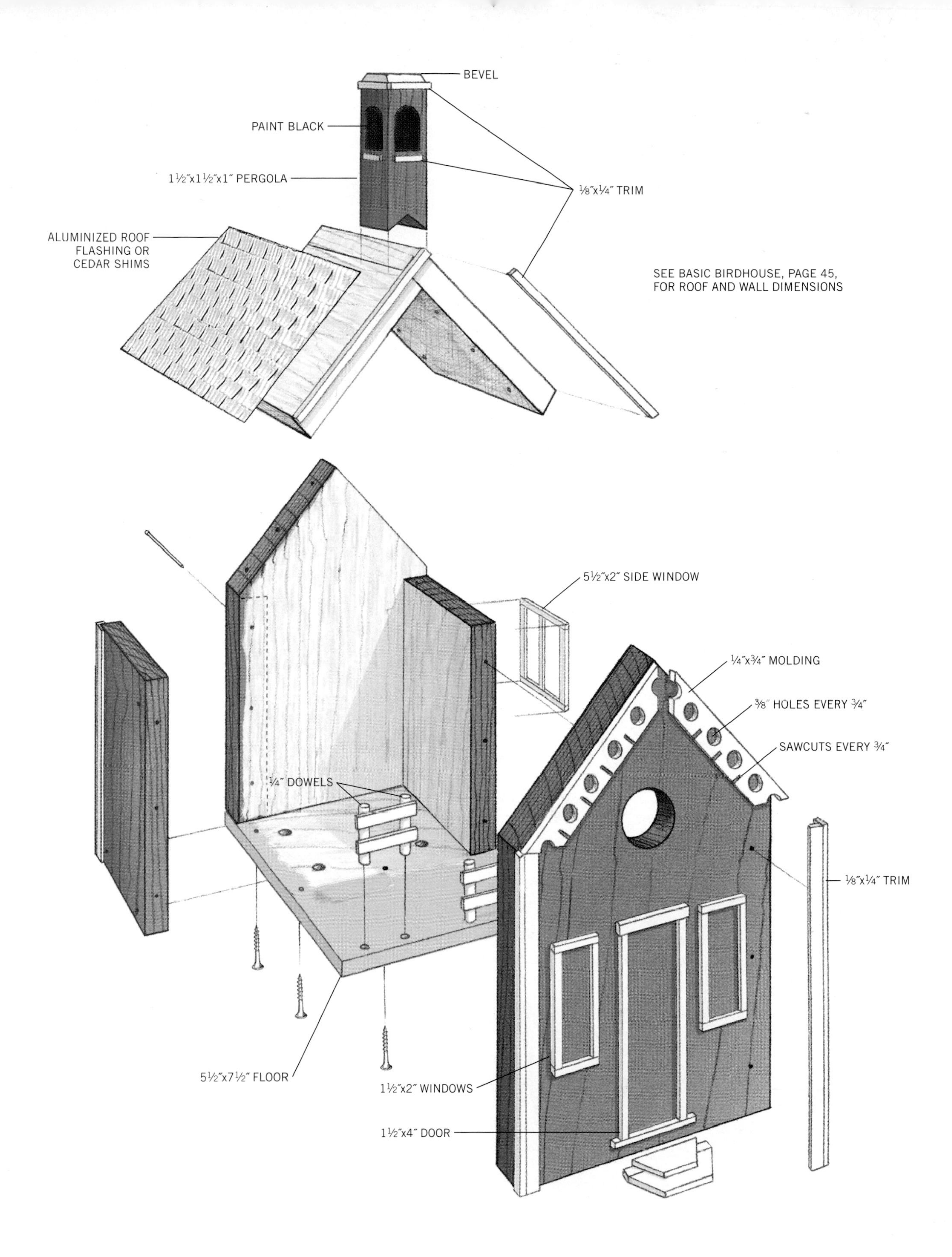
BEVEL
PAINT BLACK
1½"x1½"x1" PERGOLA
⅛"x¼" TRIM
ALUMINIZED ROOF
FLASHING OR
CEDAR SHIMS
SEE BASIC BIRDHOUSE, PAGE 45,
FOR ROOF AND WALL DIMENSIONS
5½"x2" SIDE WINDOW
¼"x¾" MOLDING
⅜" HOLES EVERY ¾"
SAWCUTS EVERY ¾"
¼" DOWELS
⅛"x¼" TRIM
5½"x7½" FLOOR
1½"x2" WINDOWS
1½"x4" DOOR

Mock Tudor

As if it came straight out of the Cotswolds, this half-timbered cottage puts a Renaissance face on the Basic Birdhouse. Build it to be a display piece or use it outdoors, since it is quite rugged. Best of all, it's deceptively easy to build. The plastering stage is especially fun for kids.

First build the Basic Birdhouse, as discussed on pages 43–45. Then add the accouterment.

PREPARE THE PARTS

Most any molding will do for the half-timbers, as long as it's about ¾ by ¼ inch. Or, you can simply rip ¼-inch-wide pieces from 1-by stock. With a rasp, knife, or electric sander, roughen one face of the molding to simulate hand-hewn timber.

Cut the 1 by 3 in half and glue it together to form the chimney. When it's dry, cut the bottom at a 45-degree angle to fit on the roof. With a utility knife, whittle the chimney into a roughly tapered shape, then glue and nail it to the roof. ➤

This Basic Birdhouse is transformed into a Cotswolds cottage by cocoa mat and plaster.

MATERIALS

- Basic Birdhouse (see page 43)
- ¾-by-¼-inch flat molding: 8 feet
- 1-by-3 pine or other softwood: 8 inches
- Plaster patching compound
- Cocoa-mat basket liner: 12 by 18 inches
- Exterior wood glue
- Fine sandpaper
- Oil-based stain: walnut or similar color
- Spray polyurethane exterior finish: clear satin

TOOLS

- Basic hand tools
- Sponge
- Jigsaw, coping saw, band saw, or scroll saw
- Electric drill, bits, and spade bit or hole saw for entry hole

OPTIONAL: Table saw, electric sander

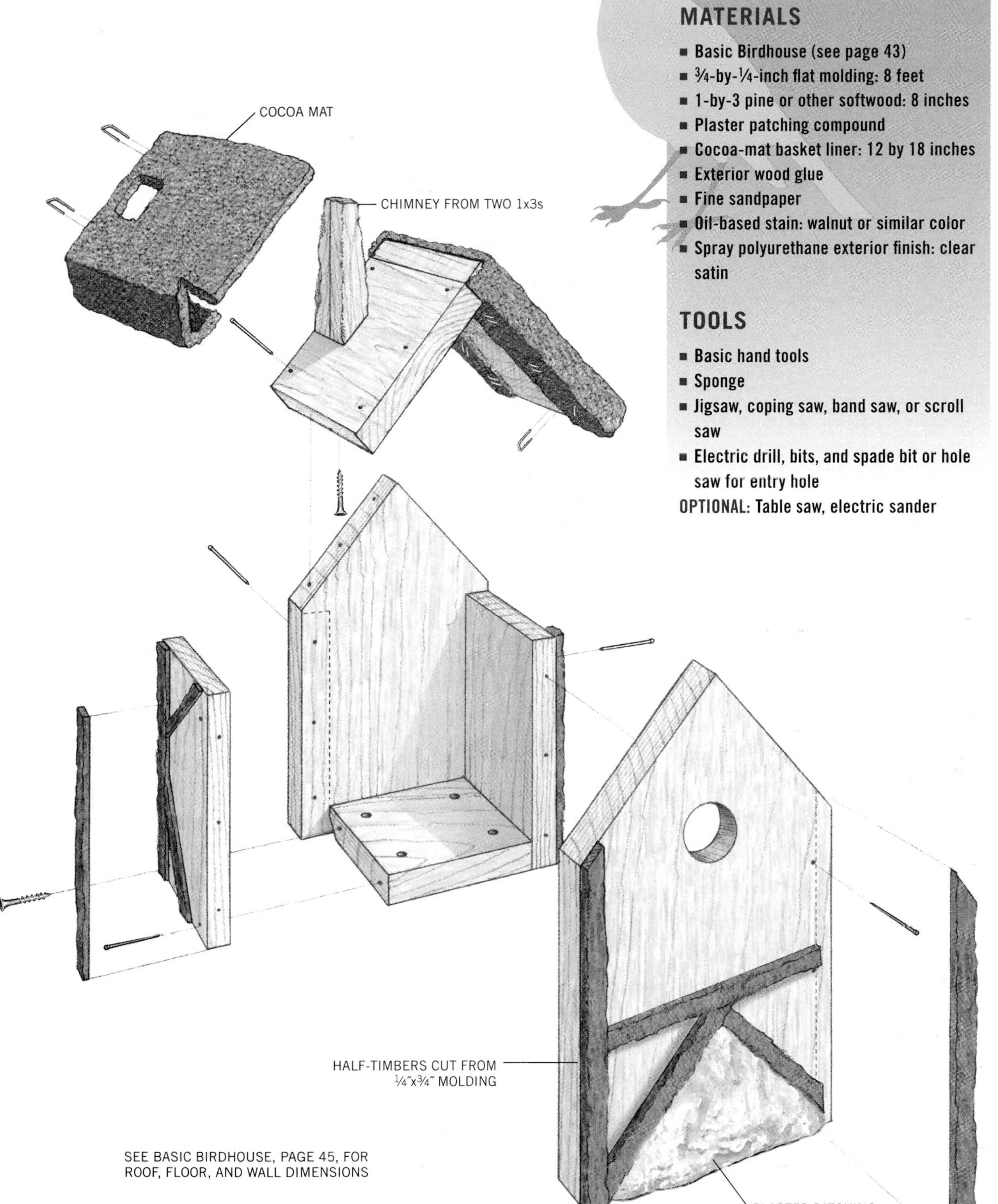

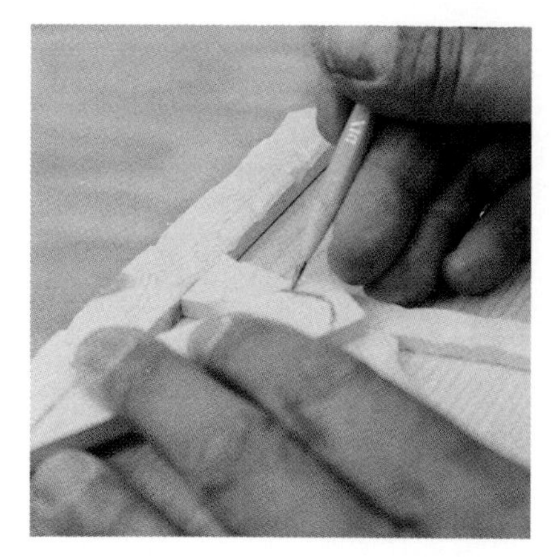

Mark the overlaps of the diagonal braces with the crosspieces, then cut the arcs.

Spread the plaster, thicker where it meets the timbers, thinner in the middle.

Notch the mat, trim it to the pencil lines, and staple on the underside of the eaves.

Position the roof on the house and trace the house outline on the underside of the roof with a pencil.

MAKE HALF-TIMBERS

Glue molding to each corner as shown in the illustration on page 51.

Next, cut main crosspieces for each house wall, but don't cut the ends square since you want the crosspieces to lie at an angle. With a coping saw (or scroll saw or jigsaw mounted upside down in a padded vise) cut shallow arcs on both sides of each crosspiece. Distress all exposed square edges with a rasp or sander, then glue the crosspieces in place.

Now cut three or four diagonal braces for each panel, marking overlaps as shown above. Cut arcs in these pieces, distress the edges, and then glue them in place.

All this work can be done quite casually and quickly. The rougher the pieces and their joinery, the more charming the house.

Stain the timbers after all are attached. Don't worry about getting stain on the walls since the plaster will cover it.

PLASTER THE WALLS

For each wall, place about a half cup of patching plaster in a disposable cup. Stir with a stick while adding enough cold water to make a slurry about as thick as heavy pancake batter. Now you've got about ten minutes to place plaster in each half-timbered space and spread it with your fingers, as shown above. Make it thicker where it meets the timbers, thinner in the middle.

Don't worry about getting plaster on the timbers. When the plaster has partially set, scrub it off the timbers with the scrubbing side of the sponge, then finish with a sponge side. Some plaster haze will remain but it will disappear under the polyurethane coat you'll apply later.

Start on the backside, and your technique will be perfect by the time you get to the front. Finish by adding some plaster to the chimney.

THATCH THE ROOF

Staple cocoa mat to the underside of the non-chimney eaves, centered end-to-end, and flush with the pencil tracing you made in Prepare the Parts. Wrap it over to the chimney side. Mark and cut an opening for the chimney, then extend the mat to the other eaves, trim to the line with scissors, and staple in place.

To complete the thatching, notch the mat as shown above, trim to the pencil lines, and staple in place on the underside of the eaves. Nail on the roof to complete your house.

Tin Shack

Charmingly ramshackle, this house uses corrugated cardboard to convincingly simulate corrugated iron siding. Minimally protected against water, it's probably best as a fair-weather birdhouse or display piece. This is a very casual project that's lots of fun to do—especially the part where you get to make your own rust!

Begin by building the Basic Birdhouse, as discussed on pages 43–45. ➤

MATERIALS

- Basic Birdhouse (see page 43) with roof of ¼-inch plywood
- Corrugated cardboard: about 6 square feet
- ¼-by-¼-inch pine or balsa wood: 8 feet
- ¾-or ½-inch dowel: 6 inches
- Exterior wood glue
- Hot-melt glue
- 3d galvanized finishing nails
- ⅜-or ½-inch screw-hole button (to match dowel): 1
- Fine sandpaper
- Spray paint: flat gray primer; copper, gold, and silver metallic; flat black
- Spray polyurethane exterior finish: clear satin

TOOLS

- Basic hand tools
- Staple gun
- Electric drill, bits, and spade bit or hole saw for entry hole
- Scrub brush

OPTIONAL: Table saw, electric sander

Spray one side of the cardboard thoroughly, let soak through, then peel away the top layer.

For extra durability, cut the siding and dip it into satin polyurethane before painting.

Starting at the base of the structure, glue the siding in place, then staple the top edges.

Apply glue to each notch, wait a bit, then bend notches closed to create the crooked chimney.

MAKE THE SIDING

Spray one side of the cardboard thoroughly with water and let soak for about five minutes. Then peel away the top layer as shown top left. If any cardboard "webbing" remains, spray again, and remove it gently with a scrub brush.

PAINT SIDING & TRIM

When the cardboard is still not quite dry, start the "rust" treatment. Spray the surface unevenly with gray undercoat, letting some of the cardboard brown show through. Now start working over the surface with short bursts of metallic color (we used copper, gold, and silver, in that order) until you get the look you want. Use the flat black sparingly to add chiaroscuro. Finally, paint the trim in the same manner.

If you'd like your house to stand up to a light shower or two, before you paint it cut up the siding as shown top right (and as directed in Cut & Attach Siding). Then dip each piece in satin polyurethane and let dry on waxed paper. When dry, place all the pieces in a single layer for painting.

PREPARE THE HOUSE

Paint the house and exposed area under the roof eaves flat gray. Paint the door area flat black. Outline the door by gluing trim pieces in place as shown in the illustration opposite. Glue and nail the roof in place.

CUT & ATTACH SIDING

Cut the siding into random pieces ranging from about ½ inch to 2 inches wide and 3 to 5 inches long. Starting at the bottom of each wall, glue the siding pieces in place (hot glue for indoors, wood glue for outdoors), staple, and trim as shown bottom left. Keep things pretty square for the most part, but let the occasional panel run askew for a dilapidated effect.

Make the door from a piece of siding and glue it inside the door frame so it appears to be part way open.

Do the roof the same way you did the walls, bending the siding over the gable ends. Finally, glue narrow pieces of siding along the ridge line to hide the last staples.

MAKE THE CHIMNEY

To make the chimney, notch the dowel almost all the way through in two places, as shown bottom right. Put a drop of wood glue in each notch, let it sit a minute, then bend the notches closed. Glue the screw button on top.

Paint the chimney flat black, then "rust" it with the metallic paints. Drill a hole for the chimney and glue it in place on the roof.

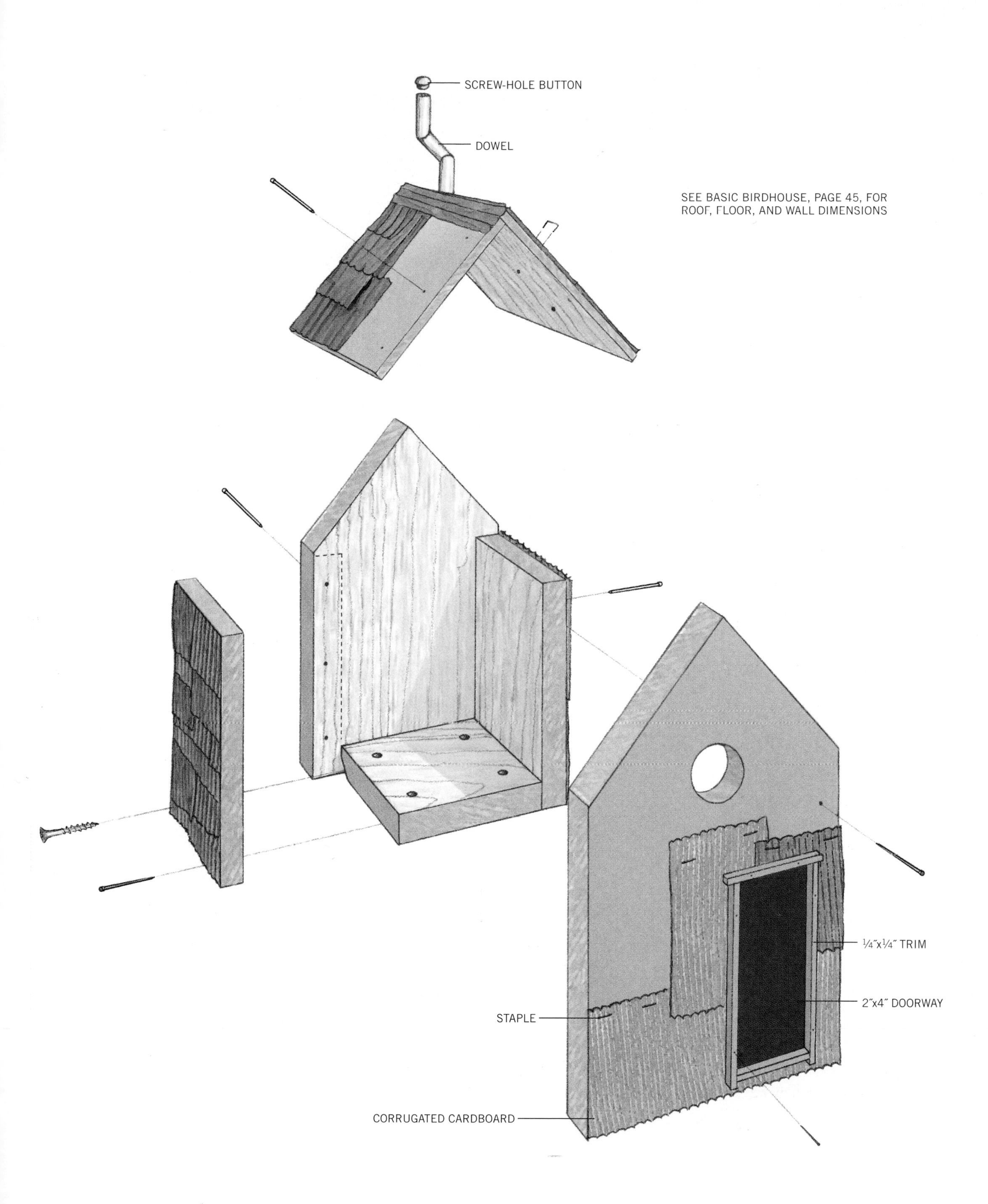
SCREW-HOLE BUTTON
DOWEL
SEE BASIC BIRDHOUSE, PAGE 45, FOR
ROOF, FLOOR, AND WALL DIMENSIONS
¼″x¼″ TRIM
2″x4″ DOORWAY
STAPLE
CORRUGATED CARDBOARD

A Touch of the East

With its decoupage walls and simple stick trim, this elegant little house evokes the serenity of Japanese architecture. Yet as prim and proper as it may be, it's not fragile and can handle the occasional shower. It's so easy to build you might consider producing a series, varying the surface treatments and the stains used on the trim.

Begin by building the Basic Birdhouse; for instructions and dimensions, see pages 43–45.

PREPARE THE PARTS

Paint the roof black. If you're using a light-colored paper or fabric for the walls, paint the house with white primer. Stain about 30 inches of the trim sticks red and about twice as much black, as shown at top right.

APPLY THE PAPER

Mix a tablespoon of wood glue with a tablespoon of water. With a foam brush, spread the thinned glue evenly on the back of the house. Align one edge of the paper with one corner and press in place. Smooth out and coat the surface of the paper with more glue.

Repeat for the other walls, trimming the paper so it overlaps the point where you started by about a half inch, as shown at middle right. When the glue is dry, cut away any excess paper, top and bottom, with a utility knife.

TRIM THE WALLS

Glue the black trim sticks to the walls and secure them with escutcheon pins in 1⁄16-inch holes, as shown at bottom right. These pieces should be about 6⅜ inches long for the Basic Birdhouse, but if you have varied your house size, check to see that this produces a slight overlap at the corners. Then, once the sticks are secured, stain the ends. ➤

Decorative paper, paint, and trim sticks give this house an Asian flavor.

Align one edge of the paper with one corner and wrap the house, adding glue as you go.

Secure the black trim sticks to the walls with escutcheon pins in 1⁄16-inch holes.

MATERIALS

- Basic Birdhouse (see page 43)
- Rice paper or other decorative paper (or fabric): 12 by 24 inches
- ¼-by-¼-inch pine or other softwood (or 14 chopsticks): 8 feet
- ⅝-inch brass escutcheon pins
- Exterior wood glue
- Fine sandpaper
- Spray paint: black; flat white primer if needed
- Water-based wood stain: black and red
- Spray polyurethane exterior finish: clear satin

TOOLS

- Basic hand tools
- Electric drill, bits, and spade bit or hole saw for entry hole
- Small foam brush

OPTIONAL: Table saw, electric sander

Position the red trim sticks so they hide the nails used to attach the roof, and affix.

ATTACH THE ROOF & FINISH

Glue and nail the roof to the house with equal overlap front and back. Stagger the nails on opposite sides of the roof. Cut four red sticks of equal length so that they extend slightly below the eaves and past the roof peak. Fasten them with glue and escutcheon pins, positioning them to hide the roof's nails. Touch up with satin and apply several coats of polyurethane to the entire house.

SEE BASIC BIRDHOUSE, PAGE 45, FOR ROOF, FLOOR, AND WALL DIMENSIONS

ESCUTCHEON PIN

7″ RED TRIM STICKS

3d GALVANIZED FINISHING NAIL

DECORATIVE PAPER

NAIL ALLOWS FLOOR TO PIVOT DOWN

1½″ SCREW

BLACK TRIM STICKS

ESCUTCHEON PIN

Room and Board

Here's a rough-and-ready bed and breakfast for birds of all kinds. If you don't get a boarder, it's certain you'll get some breakfast guests. The top floor provides an ample nesting box. The bottom is a tray feeder with a lip to help contain spills.

Because construction is extra easy, the project is a good one to do with kids. Nearly the entire structure can be cut from a single 7-foot fence board. For maximum character, use a well-weathered board. The trimmings are up to you. We chose driftwood, an old faucet handle, bronze upholstery nails, artificial moss, and a "banner" made from a scrap of aluminum flashing. ➤

MATERIALS

- 1-by-8 weathered fence board: 7 feet
- Redwood lath: 8 feet
- 3d galvanized finishing and box nails
- 1¾-inch outdoor screws
- Exterior wood glue
- Hot-melt glue
- Fine sandpaper
- Spray paint: black; flat white primer if needed
- Water-based stain: black and red
- Spray polyurethane exterior finish: clear satin
- Wire for hanging
- Various trimmings: brads, old hardware, metal flashing, dowel, upholstery nails, galvanized staples, scrap wood, twigs, artificial moss

TOOLS

- Basic hand tools
- Jigsaw, coping saw, band saw, or scroll saw
- Electric drill, bits, and spade bit or hole saw for entry hole
- Small foam brush

OPTIONAL: Table saw, electric sander

CUT OUT THE PARTS

With a jigsaw, coping saw, band saw, or scroll saw, cut out the parts according to the pattern opposite. Drill ½-inch holes in the corners of the waste pieces formed by C and D to make it easier to turn the corners of these cuts.

Drill the entry hole (see page 126).

ASSEMBLE THE WALLS, BACK & FEED TRAY

Glue and nail the back wall, C, to side walls D. Place this subassembly upside down on your workbench so the gable overhangs the side. Attach the feed tray, E, to the side wall's legs (pieces D) with outdoor screws in ⅛-inch pilot holes, as shown at top left.

ATTACH THE GABLE, FLOOR & ROOF

Attach the front wall, C, with glue and finishing nails, as shown at top right.

Add the pivoting floor, F, as shown in the illustration opposite, by drilling ⅛-inch holes in the sides, then driving finish nails through the holes into the floor. Add the latch after the house is trimmed.

Glue and nail roof piece B in position on the gables, then nail roof panel A to the gables, as shown at bottom left, then nail A to B.

ADD THE TRIMMINGS

The tray rim and decorative band are made of redwood lath. To add them, first scribe the lath against the sides, cut and nail on; then scribe the front and rear, cut and nail on. Your B&B is now ready for decorating.

We left ours unfinished and added the details you see.

The wreath for the entry hole is made from a couple of feet of rolled up willow secured to the wall with galvanized staples.

The banner is aluminum flashing rolled around a dowel, painted, lettered with a permanent marker, then threaded through an old faucet handle and glued into a hole drilled into the front of the house.

The house and tray are trimmed with driftwood that was hot-glued then secured by nails driven into pilot holes. Bits of artificial moss were hot-glued for a final touch.

Attach the feed tray to the side wall's legs using outdoor screws driven into pilot holes.

Use 3d galvanized finishing nails to attach the front of the house to the side walls.

Nail the short side of the roof in place, then the overlapping side.

For maximum stability, the iron-and-copper cable is attached at the ends of the ridge line.

CREATE THE CABLE

The iron-and-copper "cable" shown is easy to make and adds a nice touch to this—or to any—hanging birdhouse.

Cut 2 feet of iron or steel wire, double it, and clamp the free ends in a vise. Chuck a bent nail in an electric drill, hook the head in the wire loop, pull tight, and wind it up until it looks good. Next, make a similar loop of 16-gauge copper wire, hook it on the nail, hold its other end with pliers, pull tight, and wind all the strands together.

Nail the loop end of the cable to one side of the ridge line, as shown in the photo at bottom right above. Trim the other end to the length desired, make a loop, twist it closed with pliers, and nail it in place on the opposite side of the ridge line.

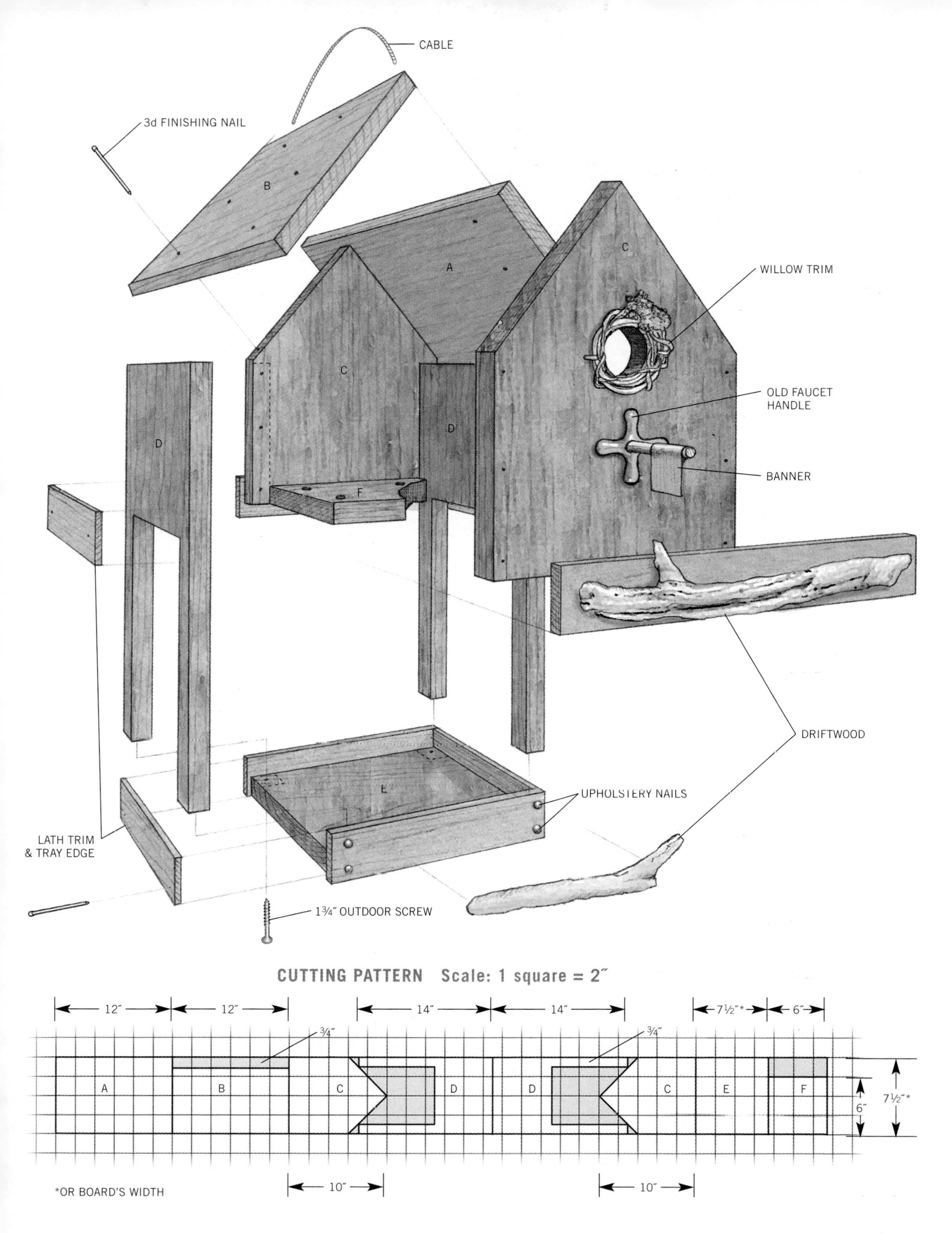
CABLE
3d FINISHING NAIL
B
A
C
C
WILLOW TRIM
OLD FAUCET HANDLE
BANNER
D
D
F
DRIFTWOOD
E
UPHOLSTERY NAILS
LATH TRIM & TRAY EDGE
1¾″ OUTDOOR SCREW
CUTTING PATTERN Scale: 1 square = 2″
12″
12″
14″
14″
7½″*
6″
¾″
¾″
A
B
C
D
D
C
E
F
6″
7½″*
10″
10″
*OR BOARD'S WIDTH

Artful Lodging

Abstract Expressionism meets Cubist forms and a Jackson Pollock paint job in this exuberant birdhouse.

Visually striking, it's a box with an attitude—in fact, any attitude you want to give it. It's easy to achieve the results shown here, but the design invites innovation as well.

Assembly is simple; the trickiest part is making sure the front and back are exactly even with each other. Follow the directions carefully and you won't have any trouble.

PREPARE THE PARTS

Enlarge the front/back pattern below right by 400 percent, then stick the copy onto the 1-by-10 wood with spray adhesive or rubber cement.

With a coping saw, jigsaw, or scroll saw, cut out front A, then use it to trace and cut out back B. Peel or sand off the paper pattern.

Cut out pieces C, D, E, F, and G from the 1 by 6. Cut roof piece H from the 1 by 8. Cut notches in piece E as shown in the illustration on page 65; these will serve as a "ladder" to permit fledglings to climb out.

BUILD FRONT, SIDES & ROOF

On the inside of pieces A and B in turn, position liner E ⅞ inch in from the inmost edge of the zig-zag side. With a pencil, trace the vertical edges of E onto both A and B; these will serve as guidelines for sides C and D.

With glue and two drywall screws, fasten piece E to the inside of front A, aligning it carefully along the lines and setting its top corners flush with the top edges of A. Drill the entry hole through the A/E subassembly.

Glue and nail sides C and D to back B, aligning their inner edges with the guidelines and setting their tops ¼ inch below the top of back B to create ventilation spaces. ➤

MATERIALS

- 1-by-10 pine or other softwood: 3 feet
- 1-by-8 pine or other softwood: 1 foot
- 1-by-6 pine or other softwood: 4 feet
- 1-inch drywall screws: 2
- 1½-inch outdoor screws
- ⅜-inch wood screw-hole buttons: 3
- 3d galvanized finishing nails
- Spray adhesive or rubber cement
- Fine sandpaper
- Oil-based paint: flat black, yellow, red, and blue
- Black permanent marker
- Spray polyurethane exterior finish: clear satin

TOOLS

- Basic hand tools
- Jigsaw, coping saw, band saw, or scroll saw
- Electric drill, bits, and spade bit or hole saw for entry hole

OPTIONAL: Table saw, electric sander

FRONT/BACK PATTERN Scale: 1 square = 1″

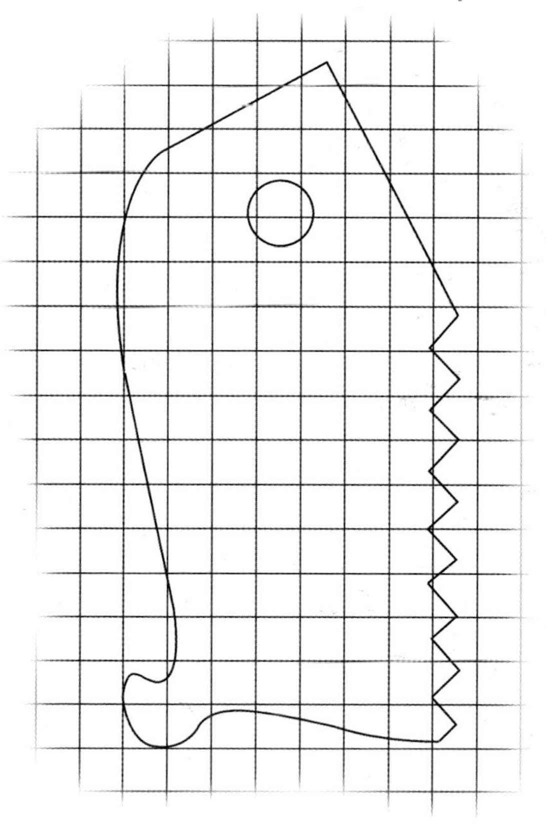

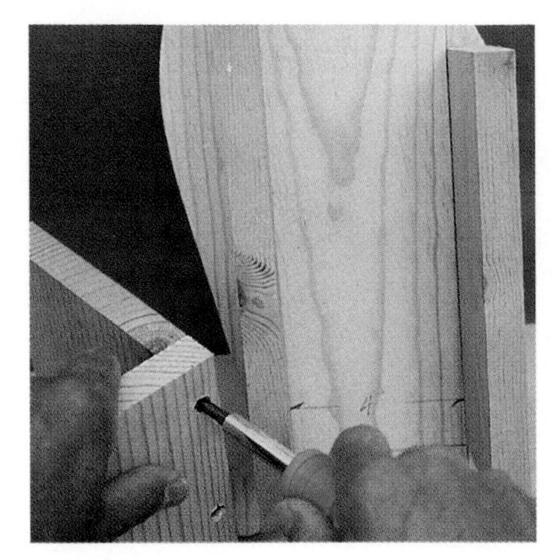
Fasten the roof pieces together with outdoor screws set in counterbored holes.

Stick masking tape to the front, then cut out irregular shapes with a razor knife.

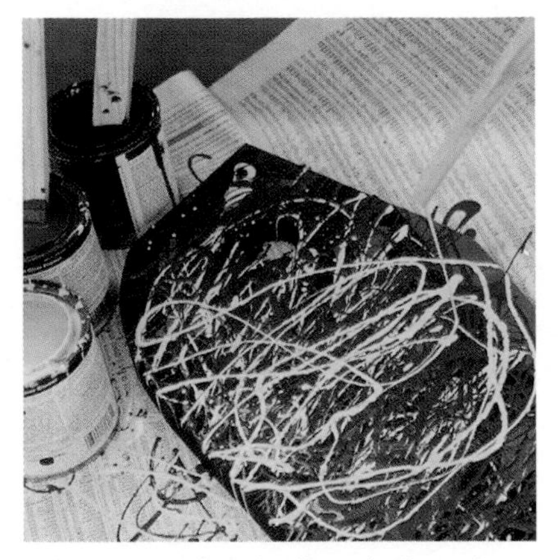
Drizzle blue, red, and yellow—in that order—oil-based paint over the front surface.

Fasten floor F to liner E with two outdoor screws, then remove it and set aside. Align A/E with B, then drill ⅛ inch pilot holes in sides C and D. Fasten A/E to the sides with outdoor screws, then remove for painting.

Fasten roof pieces G and H together as shown above, using three outdoor screws set in ⅜-inch counterbored holes about 3⁄16 inch deep.

Paint all surfaces of these subassemblies that will show when the house is finished with flat black paint. Paint the screw-hole buttons yellow.

DECORATE & PAINT

Stick 1- or 2-inch-long pieces of painter's masking tape to the front, then cut out irregular shapes with a razor knife, as shown top middle.

Then, using stirring sticks, drizzle the three primary colors over the surface in random, Jackson Pollock–like patterns, as shown top right. We found it best to start with blue, then go to red, then to yellow. Moving quickly, we made two passes with this color sequence, taking extra care to leave an edge of each tape shape exposed for easy removal.

After only 15 minutes or so, lift the edges of the masking tape with a razor knife and pull the shapes off. Work carefully so you don't smear your masterpiece. Let the paint dry.

Using a foam brush, paint the edges of the house in the primary colors. If you slop over onto the black paint, just touch up those areas with more black paint; for minor fixes, simply use a black marker once the paint has dried.

COMPLETE THE ASSEMBLY

When all the paint has thoroughly dried (waiting overnight is best), carefully refasten A/E to the house sides with four outdoor screws. Screw floor F in place with two outdoor screws.

Position the roof on the house, then drill a 1⁄16-inch pilot hole at the end of each gable and nail the roof in place with 3d finishing nails, setting the nailheads slightly below the surface, as shown right. Touch up with paint or a marker, then glue on the yellow screw-hole buttons

Spray the entire house with satin polyurethane or marine varnish to protect your artwork.

Nail the roof in place with finishing nails, setting the nailheads slightly below the surface.

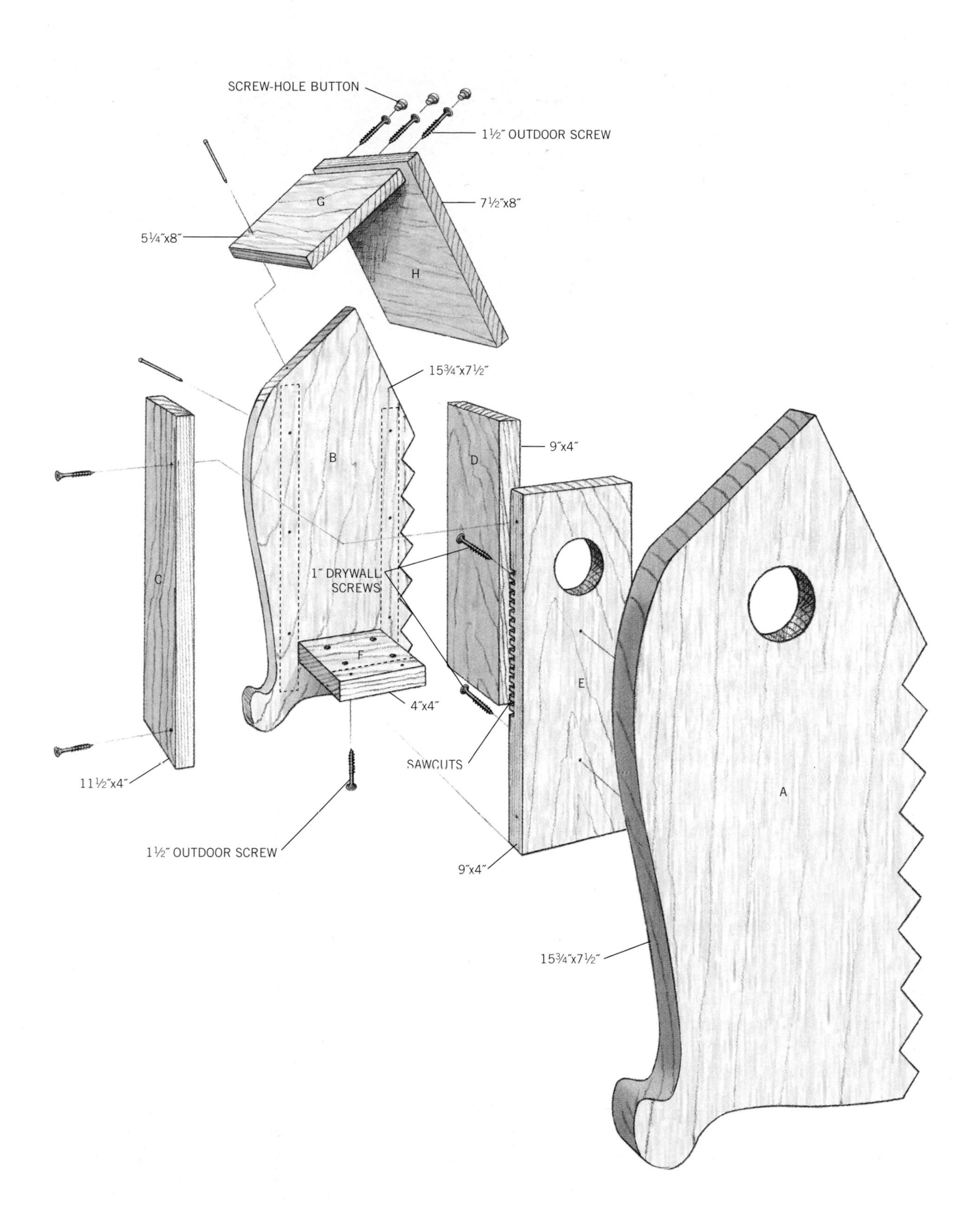
SCREW-HOLE BUTTON
1½″ OUTDOOR SCREW
G
7½″x8″
5¼″x8″
H
15¾″x7½″
B
D
9″x4″
C
1″ DRYWALL SCREWS
F
E
4″x4″
A
11½″x4″
SAWCUTS
1½″ OUTDOOR SCREW
9″x4″
15¾″x7½″

Castle Keep

Seeming straight out of the Middle Ages, this formidable tower is actually a friendly fortress for birds. Construction components are flexible, easy to use, and inexpensive—just plaster over an armature made of wood, plastic pipe, and hardware cloth (wire mesh).

You don't have to be detail-oriented to build this one, and the design freely lends itself to adaptation. Working with the plaster provides a messy satisfaction, so kids have a lot of fun joining in. The surface is weatherproof enough for the nesting season in most locales, but no matter where you live, don't leave it out all winter.

MATERIALS

- 1-by-10 pine or other softwood: 2 feet
- 4-inch (inside diameter) ABS or PVC plastic pipe: 1 foot
- Redwood lath: 1 foot
- ¼-inch mesh hardware cloth: one 3 by 17 inches and one 14 by 17 inches
- 3d galvanized nails
- Hot-melt glue
- Corrugated cardboard
- 16-gauge wire
- Plaster patching compound: 3 pounds
- Brass eye screws: 4 (small)
- ⅝-inch brass escutcheon pins
- Brass chain
- Trimmings: twigs, artificial moss, etc.
- Spray paint: flat black, moss green, rust, and faux sandstone finish
- Spray polyurethane exterior finish: clear satin

OPTIONAL: Aluminum flashing, small wood dowel

TOOLS

- Basic hand tools
- Jigsaw, coping saw, band saw, or scroll saw
- Electric drill, bits, and spade bit or hole saw for entry hole
- Hot-melt glue gun
- Disposable latex gloves

PREPARE THE PARTS

Cut out the base, two top circles, and the 12 blocks for the crenelations from the wood. Bevel the top edge of the base. With tin snips, cut the hardware cloth; make 3-inch cuts, spaced every 2 inches, along one long edge of the larger piece.

Drill the entry hole in the pipe. Hot-glue the lath—which will become a climbing strip for nestlings—to the interior of the pipe, running it from the lower edge of the hole to the bottom, then trim the excess.

MAKE THE BASIC ARMATURE

Roll the larger piece of hardware cloth tightly around the pipe; let it spring back, then remove it and set it aside.

Hot-glue the pipe to the center of the base. Take the mesh cylinder and bend the flaps outward 90 degrees. Then place the mesh over the pipe, overlapping the edges at the back, opposite the entry hole. Run wire around the top edge and twist to fasten the mesh tightly to the pipe.

Spread the mesh at the base and staple the flaps to it. Trim the overlapping edges at the back and wire them together. Hot-glue the top disks together, then to the top of the pipe.

Staple the smaller piece of hardware cloth around the disks, letting it overhang the pipe below. With a hammer, gently form the mesh so that it is flush with the disks and the pipe. Run wire around the lower edge of this mesh piece and twist at the back to fasten. Trim all wire twists and bend them flush with the pipe.

ADD THE ARMATURE DETAILS

To add the crenelations to the top, start by drawing a line across the center of the top disk, then another at 90 degrees to it. Glue four blocks to the edge of the disk, each one centered on a line. In each of the quadrants formed, hot-glue two blocks, spaced evenly. Then drill a 1⁄16-inch hole through the top of each block into the disk below and fasten with a 3d nail.

Cut away the mesh where it overlaps the entry hole. Insert a pair of pliers in the opening and, pressing firmly, rotate to smooth away the mesh from the edges. Hammer the mesh so it sits flush to the base, then hot-glue scrap blocks of wood around the base to make "boulders."

To finish, cut pointed window frames and a square door frame from corrugated cardboard, as shown at top right, and hot-glue them to the mesh.

PLASTER THE WALLS

Mix two cups of patching plaster with water until it's the consistency of very thick pancake batter. Wearing gloves, apply the plaster to the armature, pressing it into the mesh, and filling between the wood blocks on the base, as shown at middle right. Let the plaster cure overnight.

PAINT THE CASTLE

Paint the entire castle flat black and let dry. Then spray with faux-stone finish, as shown at bottom right, letting some of the black show as shadows in the hollows. Let the stone finish dry overnight, then use the rust and green to add texture and detail. Paint the interior of each window and the doorway flat black. ➤

Cut window frames and a door frame from corrugated cardboard and hot-glue to the mesh.

Apply the plaster by pressing it into the structure until all of the mesh is just covered.

After painting the castle black and allowing to dry, spray it with faux-stone finish.

"Landscape" with bits of moss, twigs, or model-train materials to suit your fancy.

ADD FINISHING DETAILS

Make the drawbridge from small pieces of wood joined with hot glue and escutcheon pins cut so they do not protrude. Fasten the drawbridge to the castle with eye screws and chain, and glue its lower edge to the doorway.

As shown above, hot-glue artificial moss, twigs, and other details to the surface to suit your fancy. If you wish, make a banner from a scrap of aluminum flashing by rolling one edge around a dowel, then painting it with royal colors. Paint or stain the dowel, drill a hole in the top of the castle for the flagpole—and raise the flag.

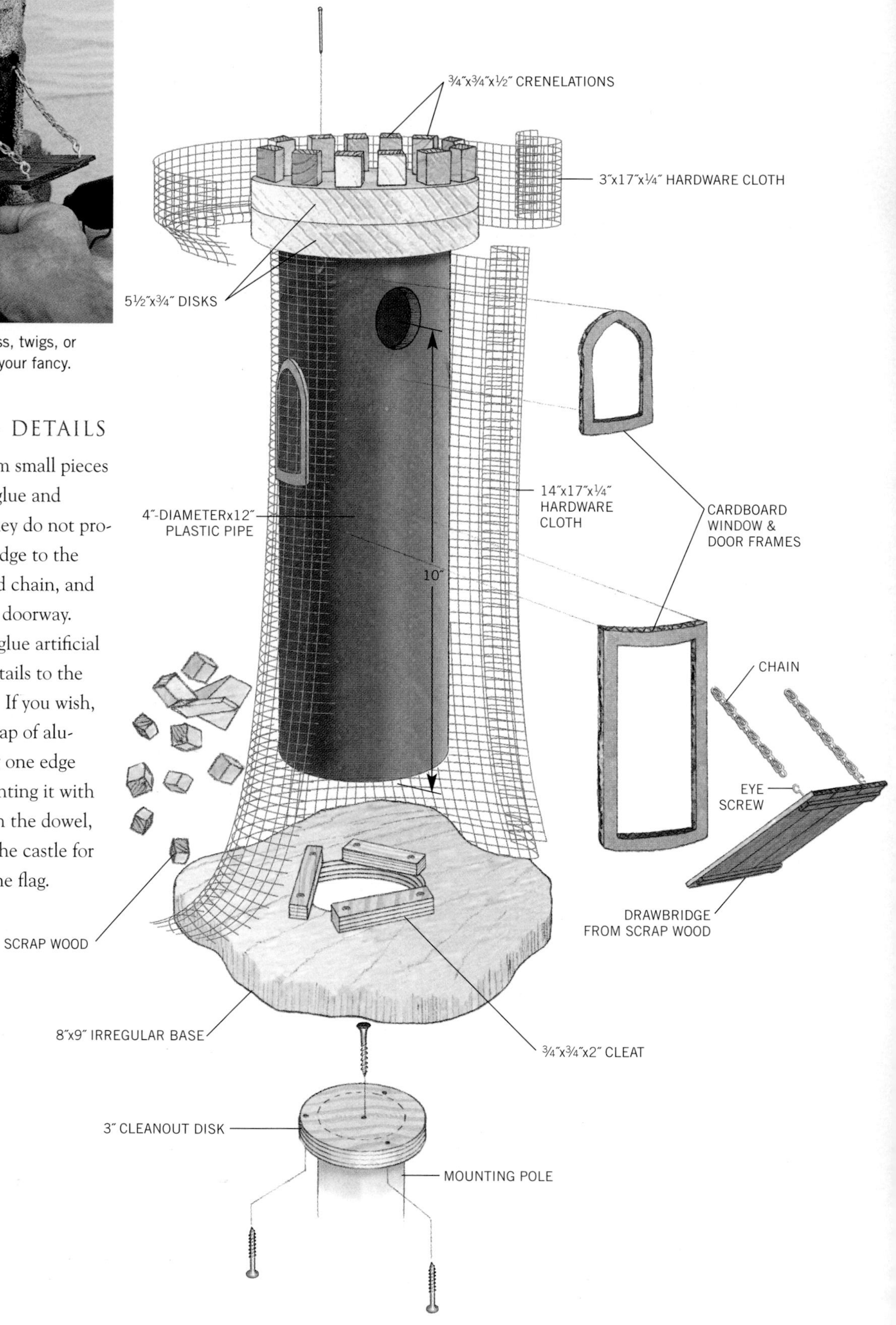

FAIRY TALE COTTAGE

Pretty enough to adorn your living room, this fantasy dwelling is also sturdy enough to make a quaint home for birds.

Special features abound: a swooping compound curved roof with chimney, convincing half-timbering, real stonework, and more. Best of all, these effects are easy to achieve, don't require a high level of craftsmanship, and finish work is almost nil. Use the patterns on page 73 and the project becomes simpler still.

For a whimsical birdhouse that looks like it came straight out of Hans Christian Andersen, give this one a try. ➤

MATERIALS

- ¼-inch plywood: 2 square feet
- 1-by-12 pine or other softwood: 1 foot
- 1-by-8 pine or other softwood: 1 foot
- 1-by-6 pine or other softwood: 1 foot
- 1-by-3 pine or other softwood: 2 feet
- ⅛-inch lauan door skin plywood: 2 square feet
- Pine lath: 3 feet
- ⅜-inch dowel: about 2 inches
- Cocoa-mat basket liner: 12 by 26 inches
- Plaster patching compound
- 1-inch drywall screws: 4
- 1½-inch drywall screws: 2
- 3d galvanized finishing nails
- ⅝-inch brads
- 16-gauge wire
- Exterior wood glue
- Silicone sealant
- Fine sandpaper
- Aquarium or pea gravel: ¾ cup
- Tempera paint: yellow, red, blue, and white
- Black permanent marker
- Spray polyurethane exterior finish: clear satin

Though there are several wooden parts to this project, cutting and shaping them is made easy with a jigsaw—and by using the patterns found on page 73.

PREPARE THE PARTS

Cut out the parts according to the illustration opposite and the patterns on page 73 (parts A, B, E, and F are shown above). Connect front A and gable B with glue and brads and drill the entry hole.

Match up the roof pieces, H, and drill four 1⁄16-inch holes through both at once along the ridge line. Sand the edges smooth, then stain the inner surfaces and edges with a dark stain. When dry, spray all surfaces and edges with several coats of polyurethane finish.

ASSEMBLE THE WALLS & CHIMNEY

Attach front A and back C to sides D with glue and 3d nails. Round off the side walls at the front left and at both rear corners to follow the contours of the front and back walls.

With a utility knife and sandpaper, whittle and shape the chimney pieces, E and F, to blend with front A, then glue filler piece G in place.

ADD THE WOOD DETAILS

With a coping saw or scroll saw, cut half-timbering from the pine lath. Cut the lower crossbeam first, following the curve of the lower edge of gable B. Distress this (and all subsequent pieces) with sandpaper, notching it and roughing it up cross-grain to simulate saw marks. Attach the piece with glue, then use it as the base for marking and cutting the other pieces.

Make the exposed ends of the beams that "support" the crossbeam from scrap wood and glue in place.

Make the bay window from a scrap of 1 by 3 and attach with glue and brads driven in from the rear.

Cut the side windows (and an optional rear window) and half-timbering from pine lath and glue in place.

With a coping saw, cut away the chimney top by cutting through piece E and front A along the line of piece F, as shown at bottom left. Sand away anything projecting above the gable line that might impede a smooth curve when you later apply the roof.

FINISH THE WALLS

Stain all wood details a dark color and allow to dry thoroughly.

Mix about a half cup of dry patching plaster to a thick pancake-batter consistency and spread it in the spaces between the gable's half-timbers. Remove any plaster from the surface of the timbers with a damp sponge. (Don't worry about leaving a slight haze; the clear finish will get rid of it.) Now proceed to the walls and chimney, mixing and applying plaster and embedding the gravel, as shown below.

Allow the plaster to cure overnight, then spray the house and upper chimney with several coats of clear satin polyurethane finish. ➤

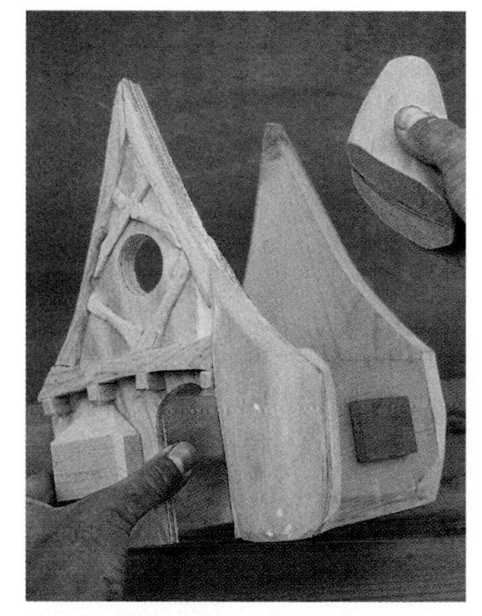
After the basic structure is assembled, cut away the chimney top along the gable line.

Apply the plaster in sections so the gravel can be embedded before drying.

TOOLS

- Basic hand tools
- Jigsaw, coping saw, band saw, or scroll saw
- Electric drill, bits, and spade bit or hole saw for entry hole
- Staple gun
- 2 or 3 clothespins or small spring clamps

OPTIONAL: Electric sander

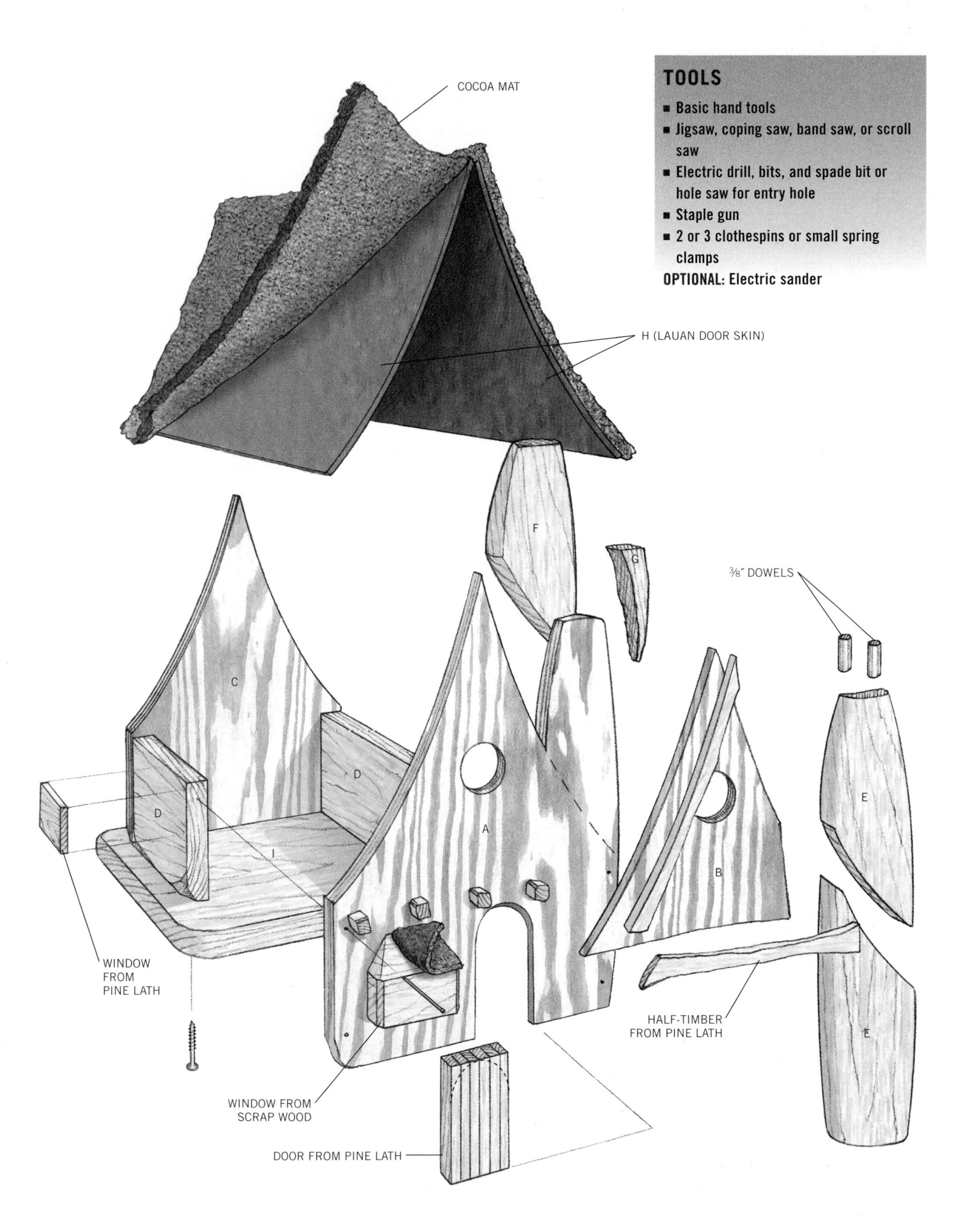

ATTACH THE ROOF & UPPER CHIMNEY

Apply a thick bead of silicone along the inner ridge line of one roof piece H and press the other piece atop it. Thread a couple of inches of wire through each ridge-line hole and twist the ends together above the gable.

Spread the roof assembly over the walls of the house and, pressing down firmly, drill ⅛-inch pilot holes, then fasten the roof in place with two 1-inch drywall screws in each gable side.

If necessary, twist the wires with pliers until the ridge line comes together and the silicone squeezes out.

Align the upper chimney section carefully and, holding it firmly in place, as shown below, attach the section with glue and two 1½-inch drywall screws (drill a ⅛-inch pilot hole from beneath through the roof and into the chimney section).

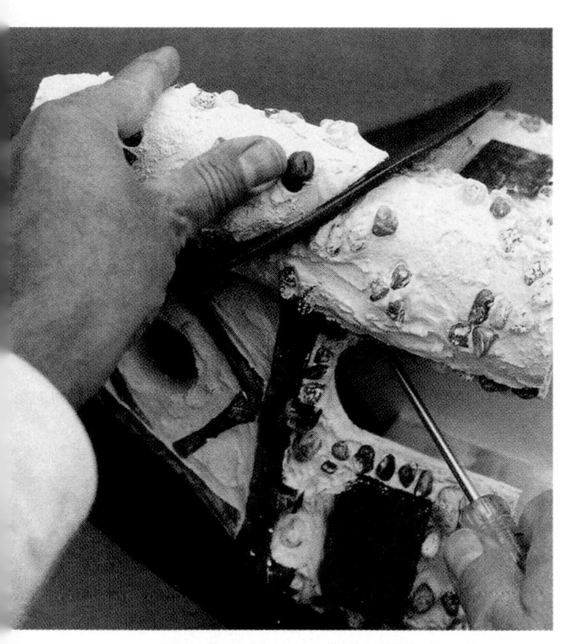

Align the chimney, drill pilot holes, then attach with glue and drywall screws.

THATCH THE ROOF

Cut the cocoa mat roughly to size. Apply silicone liberally to the left roof half, and press the mat in place. Drive staples in the center and remove them after the silicone cures. Trim the mat at the ridge line with scissors.

Make, affix, and trim the right half in the same way, as shown at right, but first cut a slot to allow the chimney to pass through the roofing.

Make a ridge piece from the cocoa mat and fasten with silicone, holding it with clothespins or spring clamps until the silicone cures.

Attach the cocoa mat to the roof with silicone, holding it in place with staples until dry.

PUT ON THE FINISHING TOUCHES

Cut a scrap of plywood to cover the doorway and clad it in wood split from pine lath. Glue the piece in place, then stain dark.

Hold the piece up to the inside of the doorway and trace the outline onto its surface. With a permanent marker, draw hinges, a doorknob, and any other details that fancy dictates. Glue the door on from the inside.

Daub pale-blue paint on all the windows in a rough diamond pattern and add white highlights here and there. Let the paint dry, then draw a diamond grid and border on each window with a permanent marker.

Whittle three pieces from pine-lath scrap for a roof over the bay window. Cover with cocoa mat and then glue in place.

Cut "chimney pots" from the ⅜-inch dowel, one an inch long and the other ¾ inch long. Chamfer the upper edges of the dowels and paint the dowels red. Drill ⅜-inch holes ¼ inch deep in the top of the chimney and glue the chimney-pot dowels in place. Spray all finishing details with satin polyurethane.

ADD THE BASE

Place the completed house on the 1 by 12 and trace its outline. Cut the 1 by 12 in an irregular shape to create a "lawn" around the cottage, allowing an inch or so projection on all sides. Paint the base a variegated green (loosely mixed yellow and blue tempera is best).

Make "blossoms" in the lawn by spattering with white paint. Dip an old toothbrush in paint, hold it a foot or so away from the base, then run a wood scrap along the bristles to make them flick the paint randomly. When all is dry, spray on several coats of satin polyurethane. Attach the base to the house with two outdoor screws driven into the side walls from beneath.

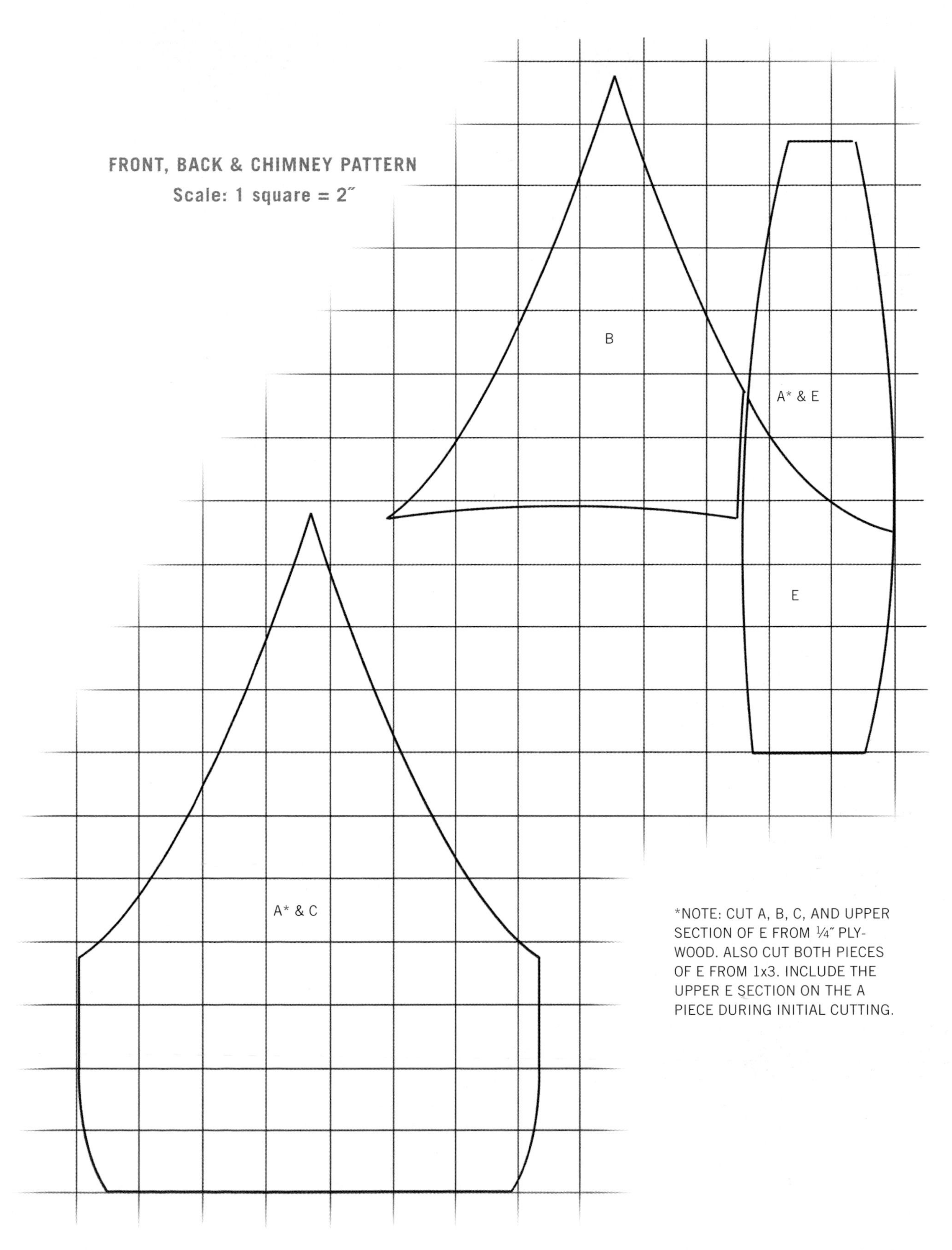

*NOTE: CUT A, B, C, AND UPPER SECTION OF E FROM ¼″ PLYWOOD. ALSO CUT BOTH PIECES OF E FROM 1x3. INCLUDE THE UPPER E SECTION ON THE A PIECE DURING INITIAL CUTTING.

Big Red Barn

As the essence of country charm, barns are a natural inspiration for the birdhouse builder. If you fancy a rural motif, this double-house design is made to order.

It's fast and easy to build—although you can while away the hours to your heart's content adding more details. A handsome, weathered finish adds authenticity. Rugged construction and a watertight roof enable the house to stay out all year long. Cleanout doors and readily adaptable proportions (see the chart on pages 126–127) make it practical for a wide range of birds.

MATERIALS

- 1-by-8 pine or other softwood: 2 feet
- 1-by-6 pine or other softwood: 3 feet
- 1½-inch plywood: 2 by 2 feet
- ¼-inch plywood: about 1 by 2 feet
- ½-by-1½-inch pine lath: 2 feet
- ⅛-by-⅜-inch batten: about 6 feet
- 3d galvanized finishing nails
- ⅝-inch brads
- Exterior wood glue
- 3-inch-wide self-adhesive roof flashing
- Fine sandpaper
- Tempera paints: red, black, and white
- Water- or oil-based paint: silver (red and black are optional for an aged roof)
- Oil-based stain: walnut or similar color
- Spray polyurethane exterior finish: clear satin

TOOLS

- Basic hand tools
- Jigsaw, coping saw, band saw, or scroll saw
- Electric drill, bits, and spade bit or hole saw for entry hole

OPTIONAL: Table saw, electric sander

PREPARE THE PARTS

Cut the ends and divider from the 1 by 8, and the sides from the 1 by 6. Mark the clearance cuts for the divider by placing the side pieces end-on in position atop the divider on each side and tracing around them. Then cut to the lines.

Drill entrance holes in each end. Cut out the plywood roof pieces and paint the edges and undersides silver.

ASSEMBLE THE HOUSE

Fasten the ends and divider to the sides with glue and 3d finishing nails, as shown bottom right.

Place this assembly atop the remaining 1 by 6 and trace inside it to mark the cleanout doors. Cut to the inside of the lines you've marked so the doors will fit easily.

Position the cleanout doors, drill ⅛-inch hinge holes through the sides only, as shown in the illustration on page 77. Drive a 3d finishing nail through these clearance holes into the doors.

To latch each door, drill a ⅛-inch hole 2 inches deep through one side into each door. Insert 3d nails to hold the doors in place. ➤

Fasten the ends and divider of this double-house design with 3d galvanized finishing nails.

Create "metal" glides for the doors and shutters from the batten material painted silver.

ADD THE DETAILS

For each end, cut two 2-by-1½-inch upper shutters and two 3-by-1½-inch lower doors from the lath. Fasten in place with glue and brads.

The rest of the trim consists of small battens measuring roughly ⅛ by ⅜ inch. You can buy small stock such as this at hobby shops, or rip it on a table saw, or cut it carefully by hand. Popsicle or crafts sticks also work well.

Add the battens to each corner, plus five or so spaced more or less evenly along the sides, fastening with glue and brads driven through 3/16-inch pilot holes in the battens.

Paint the entire assembly, plus some scrap wood, with red tempera.

Cut "metal" glides for the doors and shutters from the batten material, paint them silver, and glue in place as shown above left.

On each end, paint the entry hole and the space between the upper shutters with black tempera.

Paint the edges of the shutters and doors white, then paint Xs across them to simulate crossbracing (a foam brush with a straight, fine tip is good for this).

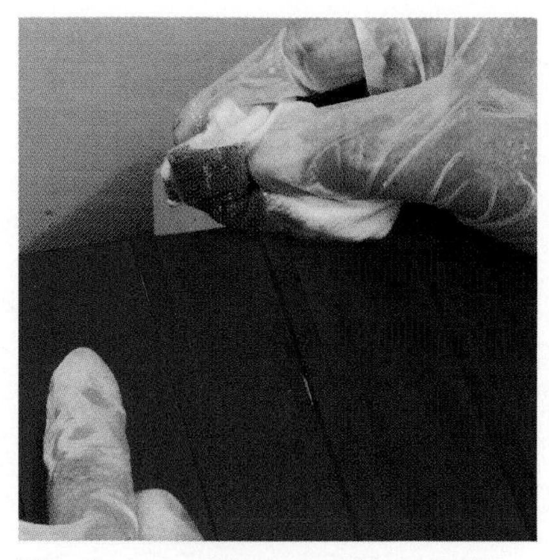

Wipe the house with a rag moistened with a dark, oil-based stain to simulate weathering.

AGE THE FINISH

To simulate wear and tear on the finish, wipe the assembly with a rag barely dampened with a dark, oil-based stain, as shown above. (Practice a bit first on the scrap wood you've painted.)

When dry, topcoat the finish with several coats of satin polyurethane.

ADD THE ROOF

Butt the roof pieces together, then glue and nail them on.

Cut the flashing material down the middle to make 1½-inch-wide strips. Lay the first strip so that it overhangs the eaves enough to wrap the edge under. Work up to the peak by laying successive strips so that they overlap each other by about a quarter inch, as shown below.

Cut a piece about 1 inch wide to run down the center of the ridge line. Roll the roofing over the gable edges and, using a straightedge and utility knife, trim it so that it overlaps the plywood by about half its thickness.

If you like, age the roof by painting it with a mixture of equal parts red and black oil-based paint and thinner, letting it sit a few minutes, then wiping with a rag until it looks "rusty."

Roof your barn with flashing material cut into strips and laid in an overlapping pattern.

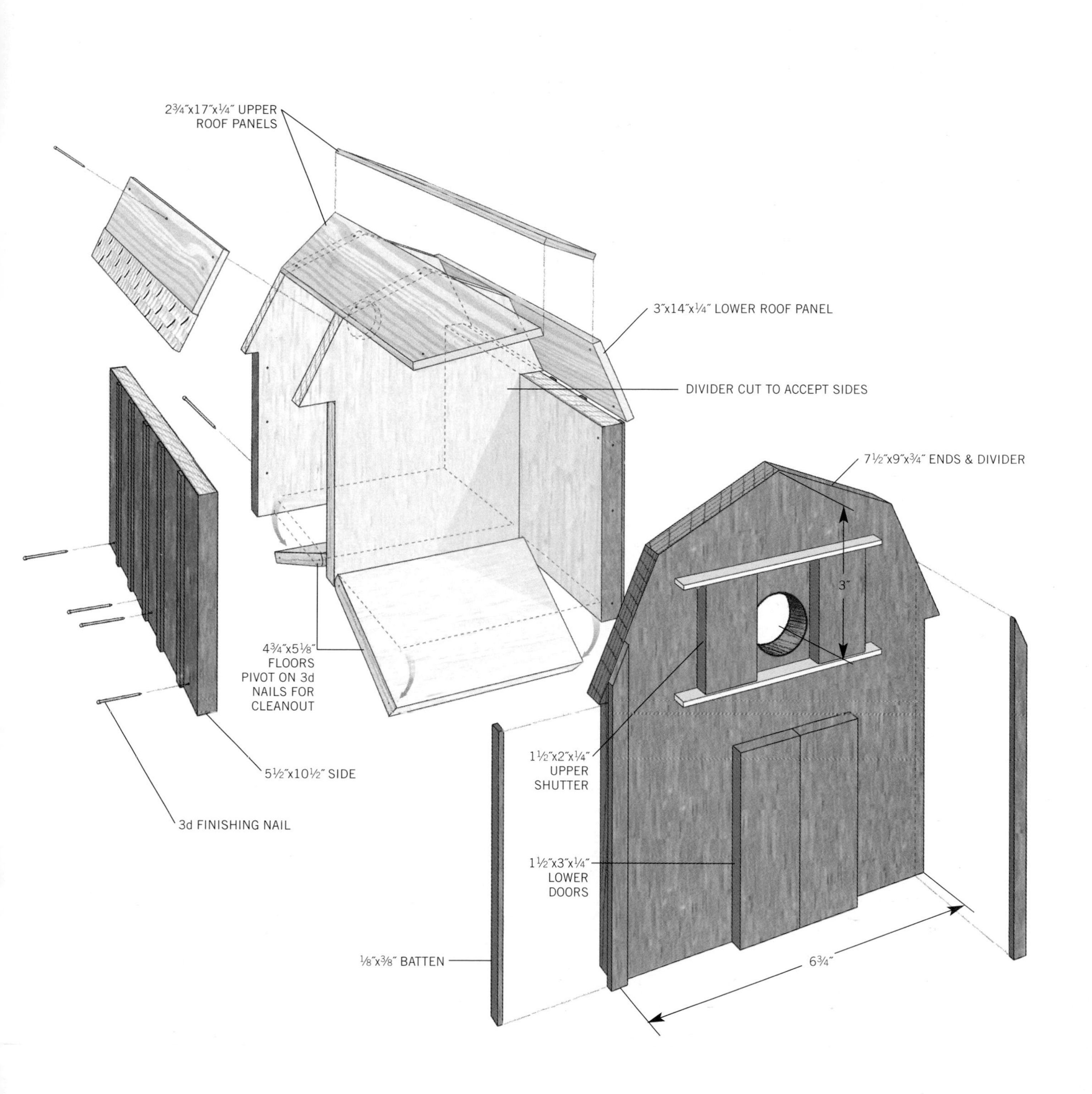

2¾″x17″x¼″ UPPER ROOF PANELS
3″x14″x¼″ LOWER ROOF PANEL
DIVIDER CUT TO ACCEPT SIDES
7½″x9″x¾″ ENDS & DIVIDER
3″
4¾″x5⅛″ FLOORS PIVOT ON 3d NAILS FOR CLEANOUT
5½″x10½″ SIDE
3d FINISHING NAIL
1½″x2″x¼″ UPPER SHUTTER
1½″x3″x¼″ LOWER DOORS
⅛″x⅜″ BATTEN
6¾″

Seashell Sand Castle

This shingled, starfish-shaped birdhouse is perfect by the seashore—or anywhere else you might want to invoke it. It makes a fine house for birds, and it's a great way to display a seashell collection. No shells? Driftwood, stones, sea glass—most any kind of flotsam—work well, too.

Construction is out of the ordinary, but very simple and completely forgiving. You need not be a carpenter nor an artist to build this one—and every one built will be unique.

You start with a frame made of dowels and plywood, cover it with cheesecloth, then add patching plaster. Shingle scraps are bent into place and whittled to a point, then the shells or other materials are grouted onto the walls. It's fun and easy.

PREPARE THE FRAME PARTS

Enlarge the pattern for the base on page 81 by 400 percent and trace it onto the plywood. With a jigsaw, coping saw, or scroll saw, cut out the base, upper and lower disks, disk spacers, and floor-hatch supports. With a rasp, bevel the edge of the upper disk as shown in the illustration on page 81. Cut the 3-inch floor hatch in the base.

Mark and drill ½-inch-diameter holes ⅜ inch deep in the base and lower disk, rocking the drill bit back and forth to widen the holes slightly for the splayed-leg construction of the frame. Cut the dowel into three 10-inch pieces and one 6-inch piece.

Plywood disks attached to a star-shaped base with dowels form the frame.

MATERIALS

- ½-inch plywood: about 2 square feet
- ½-inch dowel: 4 feet
- Cedar-shingle shims: about 20
- Cheesecloth: about 10 square feet
- Plaster patching compound: 3 pounds
- 3d galvanized box nails
- ¾-inch drywall screws: 15
- 1½-inch drywall screws: 4
- ¼-by-2-inch lag screw and washer: 1
- Exterior wood glue
- Fine sandpaper
- Sanded tile grout, sandstone color: 3 pounds
- Spray polyurethane exterior finish: clear satin

OPTIONAL: Paint or stain

TOOLS

- Basic hand tools
- Jigsaw, coping saw, band saw, or scroll saw
- Electric drill, bits, and spade bit or hole saw for entry hole
- Disposable latex gloves
- Rubber spatula

OPTIONAL: Table saw, jigsaw, electric sander

BUILD THE FRAME

Stack the upper and lower disks and spacers, and join them with glue and four 1½-inch screws.

Drill a ½-inch hole through the center of the stack and glue in the 6-inch dowel.

Connect this assembly to the base, as shown above, using glue and ¾-inch screws to fasten the long dowels in the holes you drilled in the plywood. Drill ⅛-inch pilot holes for the screws so you don't split the dowels.

Fasten the hatch supports as shown in the illustration on page 81, using glue and two ¾-inch screws for each. ➤

Copper-clad Barrel House

This whimsical little domicile made of redwood (cedar could also be used), finished in the Japanese manner with a torch and wire wheel, then clad with copper, creates a simple but striking home for small birds.

The roof arcs over the sides to keep water out, and is fully removable, so cleaning out the old nest at season's end is a snap. Though side vents keep air flowing through, it's best to place this birdhouse in the shade, either hanging as shown opposite or mounted to a fence, tree, or post, to keep its interior from becoming too warm.

Lovely when new, this simple house takes on even more character as it weathers.

MATERIALS

- 1-by-8 redwood or cedar: 16 inches
- Copper flashing: one at 8 by 9 inches and one at 6½ by 14 inches
- 3d galvanized nails
- #6-by-¾-inch round-head brass screws: 4
- ⅝-inch brass escutcheon pins
- Brass eye screws: 2
- Exterior wood glue
- 16-gauge copper wire

OPTIONAL: Silicone sealant, wood stain

TOOLS

- Basic hand tools
- Jigsaw, coping saw, band saw, or scroll saw
- Tin snips
- Propane torch
- Electric drill, bits, and spade bit or hole saw for entry hole

OPTIONAL: Wire-brush wheel and cup-shaped brush, or green patina finishing liquid

PREPARE THE PARTS

With a jigsaw or coping saw, cut out the wood ends and 3-inch-diameter security panel. For the ends, use the pattern shown on page 84, increased by 400 percent, or simply trace around a one-gallon paint can for the circle, then make a small point at the top of each piece, ¾ inch above the top of the circle.

Glue the security panel to the end that has the most interesting grain. Nail the end to the panel with 3d galvanized nails, making sure to keep the nails clear of the location of the entry hole. Drill the entry hole through both pieces.

With tin snips, cut the roof and bottom pieces from the copper flashing. Trim the roof corners and bend the copper along the ridge line as shown below right. Drill $1/16$-inch holes spaced about 1 inch apart in the edges of the bottom panel to receive escutcheon pins.

You can leave the copper roof and bottom plain, or add texture to them. We used a cup brush mounted in a drill to create the overlapping circles on the bottom of our house. See also the Honeysuckle Cottage, page 36, for a shingle-like texture, and Science Dresses Up, on page 24, for a green-patina finish. ➤

Though only two materials—redwood and copper flashing—are used to create the main parts of this project, it achieves its visual interest through simple surface treatments. A number of variations are possible.

Using a propane torch, char the surfaces of the wood ends and the security panel.

Brush away the charred wood using a wire wheel mounted in an electric drill.

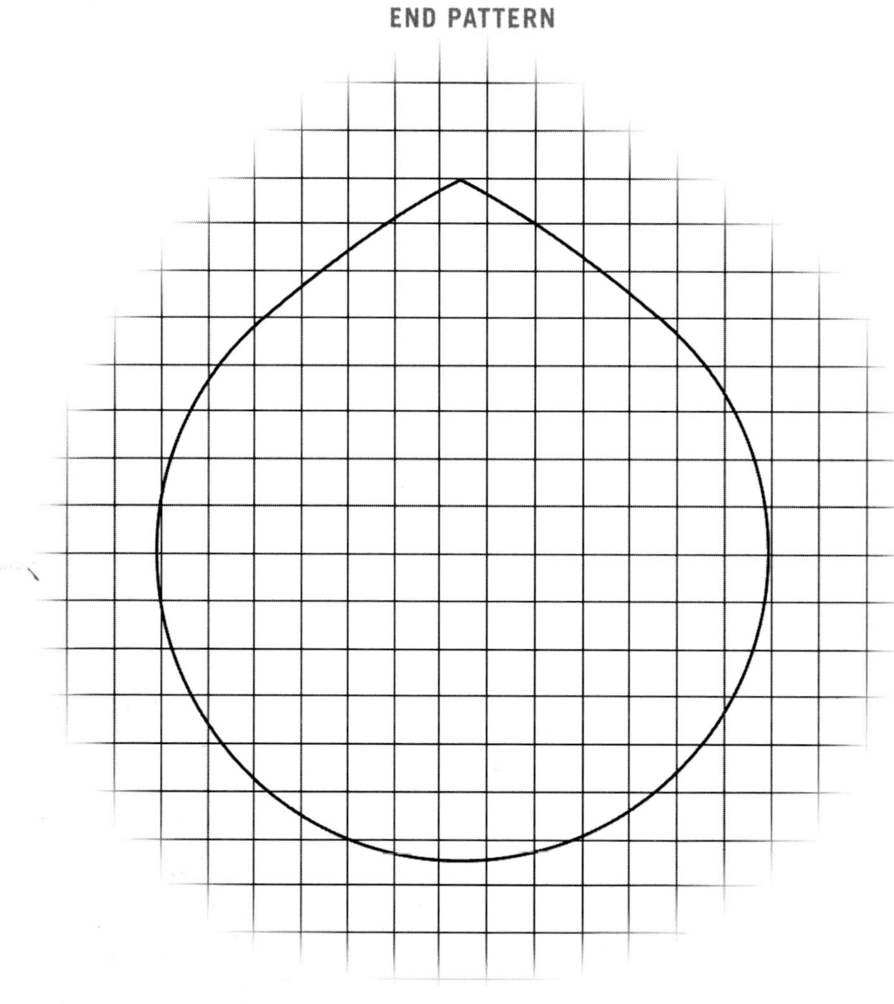

BURN & BRUSH THE WOOD SURFACE

Screw a 1-foot length of 1 by 2 or other scrap stock to the back of each end piece, and clamp the scrap in a vise. With a propane torch, char the faces of the two pieces as shown at far left. Be careful not to light the wood on fire! Keep a fire extinguisher nearby.

Mount a wire wheel in an electric drill and use it to brush away the charred wood as shown at near left. This will cause the annular rings to stand out prominently. You can accent the effect even further by staining the wood, then wiping it thoroughly.

CONNECT THE ENDS

Remove the scrap 1 by 2s, and mount one of the ends, bottom edge up, in a padded vise. Center the bottom piece of copper flashing along the end, about a quarter inch away from the front edge of the wood, as shown below. Drive brass escutcheon pins all along the edge (you'll need to unclamp the vise after driving the first half dozen or so). Repeat with the other end.

Seal the seams with silicone, applying it on the inside, but leave the bottom inch unsealed to allow for drainage.

Attach the copper flashing to the end pieces with escutcheon pins along the edge.

ADD THE ROOF

Set the roof in place so that it overhangs both ends of the copper bottom equally and the ridge is aligned with the gable peaks. Mark and drill ⅛-inch holes in the roof, front and back, halfway between the ridge line and the roof's bottom edges. Drill 1⁄16-inch pilot holes in the wood, and fasten the roof's bottom in place with ¾-inch-long brass screws.

The roof should bend and arc pleasingly over the gables but not touch the copper bottom—you want to leave about a ⅜-inch space for ventilation.

HANG OR MOUNT THE HOUSE

To hang the house, add eye screws and copper wire, as shown below. To mount it to a post or tree, remove the roof and drill a pair of pilot holes in the back. Then screw the house in place with 2-inch outdoor screws and reattach the roof. To mount it to a fence or other flat surface, insert a 1-by spacer and use 3-inch screws.

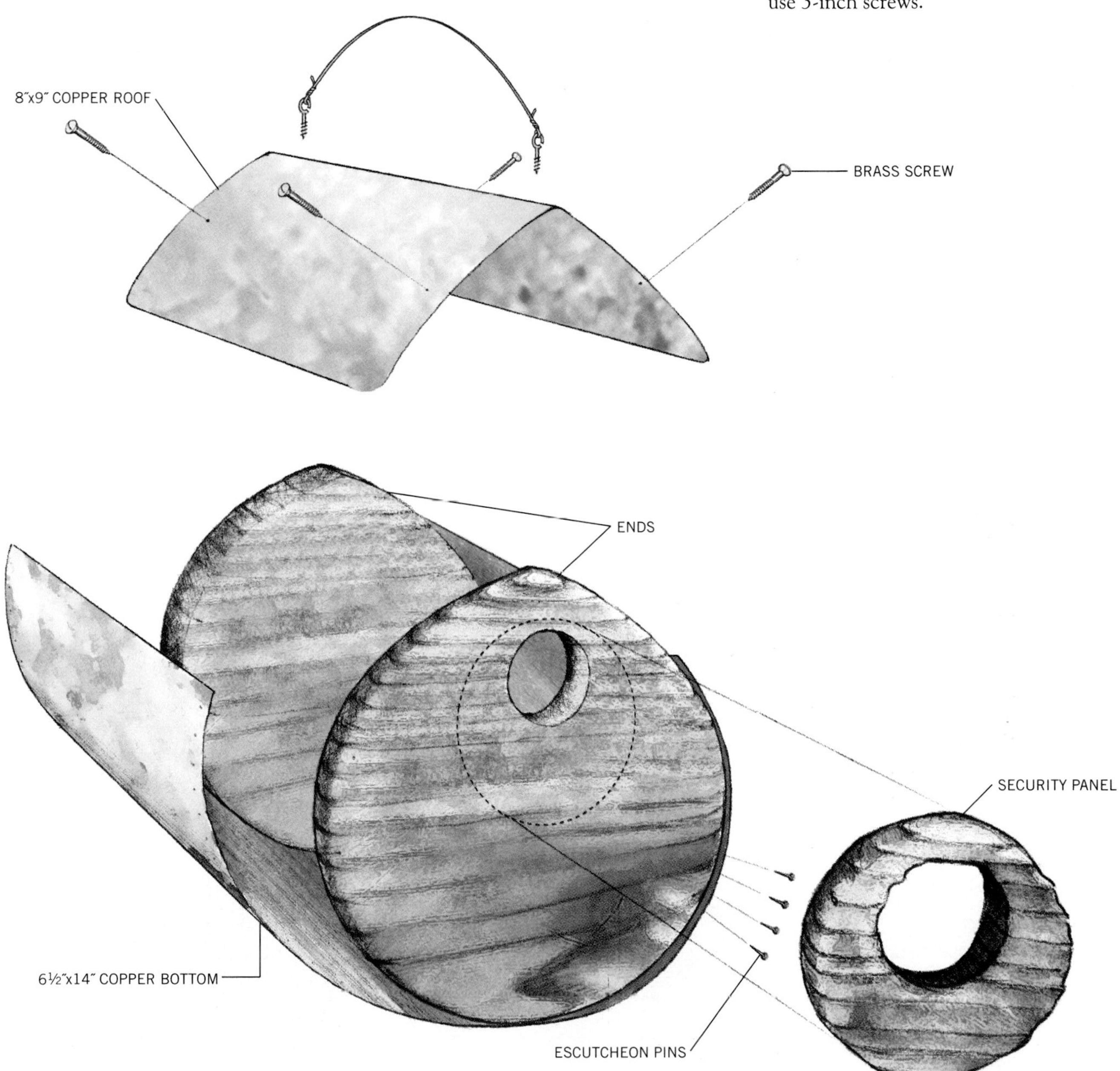

Bamboo Teahouse

This elegant two-story house adds a touch of serenity to any setting, indoors or out.

Basically just a simple box decoupaged with art papers and trimmed with bamboo, it's a fast, easy project that's also a practical home for birds. The house is well weatherproofed for the nesting season; the broad roof sheds rain, and polyurethane protects the paper.

Although the materials look rich and exotic, they're easy to come by. You'll need three kinds of rice paper or other art paper, available at art supply, crafts, or specialty paper stores. The bamboo—sold as tree stakes—is available at almost any garden center.

MATERIALS

- 1-by-6 pine or other softwood: 3 feet
- 1-by-2 pine or other softwood: 1 foot
- ¼-inch plywood: 1 by 3 feet
- 5-foot bamboo tree stakes: 3
- 3d galvanized finishing nails
- ⅞-inch outdoor screws
- Exterior wood glue
- Silicone sealant
- Fine sandpaper
- Rice paper or art paper: 1 sheet each of three kinds
- Spray enamel: flat white primer, flat black
- Spray polyurethane exterior finish: clear gloss

TOOLS

- Basic hand tools
- Jigsaw, coping saw, band saw, or scroll saw
- Electric drill, bits, and spade bit or hole saw for entry hole

OPTIONAL: Table saw, miter box, electric sander

PREPARE THE PARTS

Cut out all the parts with a handsaw, or rip the plywood with a table saw or circular saw. Paint the roof panels flat black on all sides and edges.

BUILD THE BOX

Fasten the sides to the gable ends as shown in the left top row photo. (The ¼-inch gap at the corners will hold the bamboo securely.)

Check the fit of the floors inside the box, then assemble the floor system and fasten with a single screw through one side.

Paint the entire box with flat white primer and allow to dry thoroughly.

DECOUPAGE THE WALLS

Mix two tablespoons of wood glue with an equal amount of water to create the decoupage medium.

Cut the lightest paper to fit generously around the box. Coat the back of the box with the glue mixture, position the paper, then topcoat it with the mixture. Continue in this way for the other three panels.

Trim the paper at the back so there is only a slight overlap.

Next, add torn sheets of the next darker color, positioning it dry before committing to the glue mixture.

Finish with torn sheets of the darkest color, as shown in the right top row photo. Let the paper dry thoroughly, then cut around the screw head with a utility knife.

ADD THE ROOF & CORNER POSTS

Glue and nail the roof panels in place. Using the thickest part of the tree stakes, cut the four corner bamboo posts so that they run from just under the roof to a half-inch or so past the bottom. To prevent splitting, drill ⅛-inch pilot holes through each post, about 3 inches from each end.

Slit the paper lengthwise at the corners, run a bead of silicone in the joint, then fasten the corner posts with two 3d nails each, as shown at bottom left.

FINISH THE ROOF

Cut a 14-inch piece of bamboo from the thickest remaining stock and set aside. With a pocketknife or other knife with a rigid blade, split the remainder of the bamboo by placing the knife at one end and pressing down with both hands; when you reach a node, you may need to tap the blade through with a piece of wood.

Saw the split bamboo into 6¾-inch pieces, with a 45-degree trim on one end of each piece. Starting at the ➤

Fasten the sides to the gable ends, check the fit of the floors, then assemble.

Cover the lightest paper with pieces of the next darkest color, finish with the darkest.

Drill two ⅛-inch pilot holes in each corner post, then fasten with 3d finishing nails.

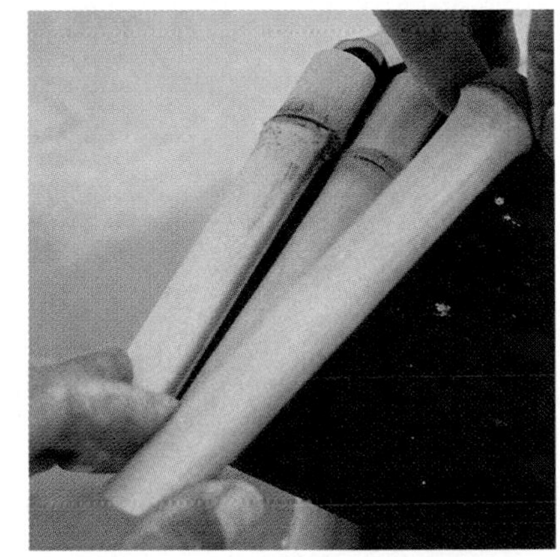

Attach the bamboo roofing pieces with silicone so the gable pieces cover the ends.

front of the roof, as shown on page 87, position two bamboo pieces to cover the gable ends of the plywood and fasten with silicone. Continue affixing the bamboo pieces until you reach the back gable, then position the rear pieces to cover the gable ends as you did for the front. Fasten the 14-inch bamboo ridge piece with outdoor screws driven into the gable ends.

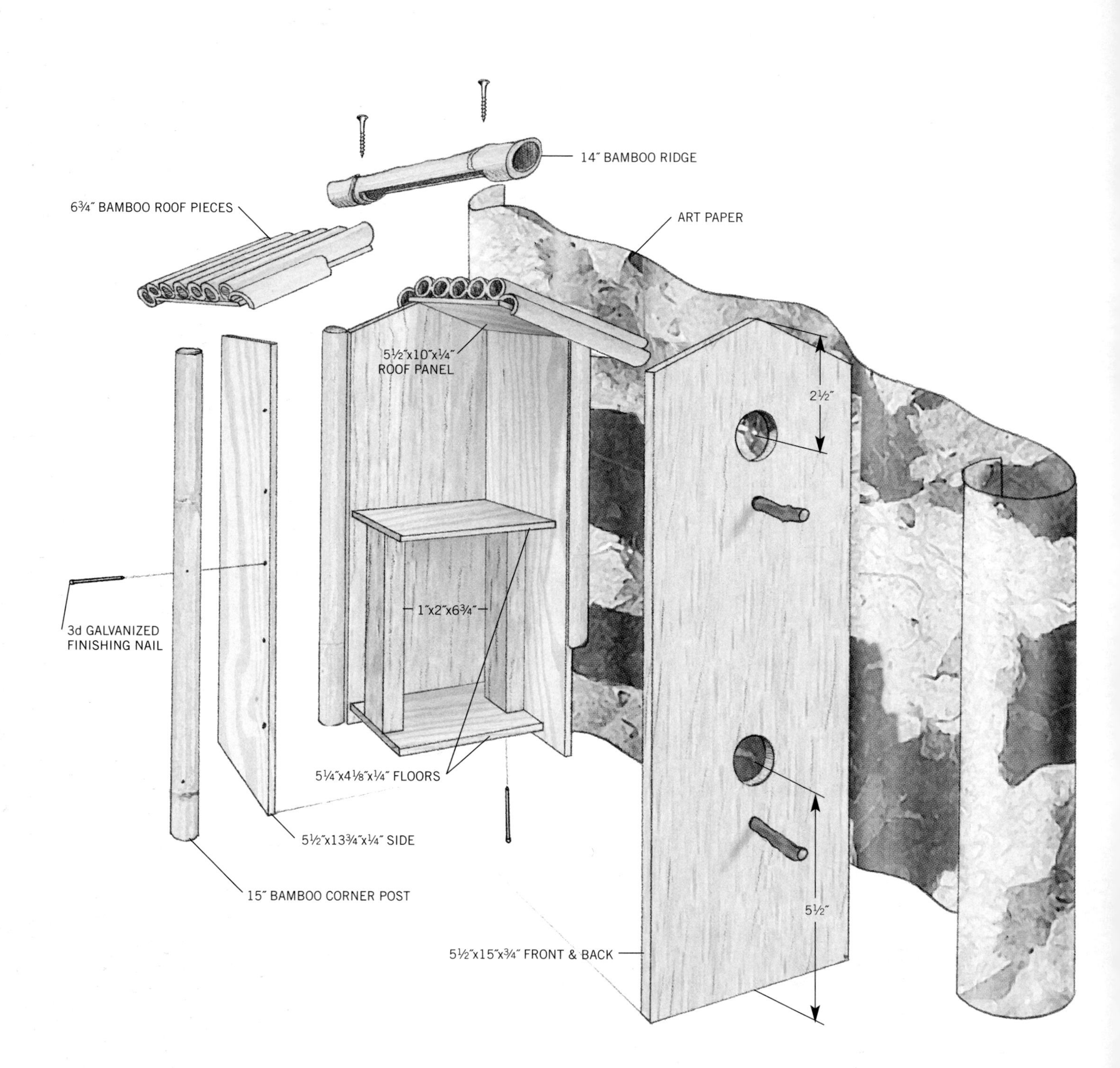

Rockin' Robin

Our salute to America's most popular instrument will gladden the heart of any music lover. All the key details of a guitar are here, but hidden inside is a birdhouse with a practical cleanout flap in back. Homemaking birds can come and go through the artfully "broken" strings.

This project takes more time than most, but it's conceptually simple, and there are no hard-to-find materials. It's as fun a way as there is to spend time in the shop, with a nice reward when you're done.

To enhance the authenticity, we've included a number of optional touches, but even without them you can still produce a really rockin' birdhouse. ➤

PREPARE THE PARTS

During the construction process, refer to the drawing on page 93. Using the pattern opposite, transfer the design for the front of the body and neck to the 1 by 12. (For authenticity, try to find a 1 by 12 with at least 14 inches of clear wood at one end; guitars don't have knots.) Cut out with a jigsaw, coping saw, band saw, or scroll saw.

To make the back of the body, trace the front's body onto the remaining piece of 1 by 12, then cut out.

MATERIALS

- 1-by-12 pine or other softwood: 4 feet
- Pine lath or similar scrap wood
- ¼- and 3⁄16-inch dowels: 1 foot each
- 4-inch galvanized flashing: 6 feet
- 3⁄32-inch brass rod: 3 feet
- ½-inch thumbscrews: 6
- ⅝-inch brads
- 3d galvanized finishing nails
- Exterior wood glue
- Silicone sealant
- 16-gauge copper wire
- Light-gauge steel wire
- Coarse and fine sandpaper
- Spray enamel: rust-color primer, flat black, white, gold
- Oil-based stain: walnut or dark color
- Spray polyurethane exterior finish: clear satin and gloss
- Masking tape
- ¾-inch black vinyl tape
- Old guitar strap or leather belt

TOOLS

- Basic hand tools
- Compass
- Colored pencils
- Black permanent marker
- Triangular file
- Jigsaw, coping saw, band saw, or scroll saw
- Electric drill, bits, and spade bit or hole saw for entry hole

OPTIONAL: Electric sander

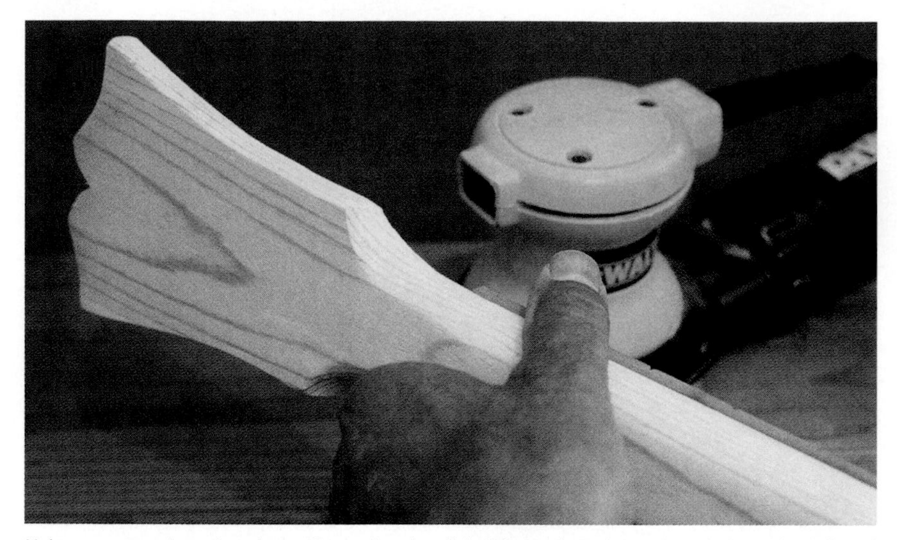

Using a rasp and sander, shape the peghead so it is thinner than the neck and slopes back from it.

Cut out the nesting-box parts, neck and tail blocks, fingerboard, bridge, saddle, and nut.

Cut bridge pins from the smaller dowel, tuner pegs from the larger. Taper one end of each bridge pin slightly with sandpaper.

Our fingerboard and bridge were cut from scraps of cedar closet lining, which is dark, so we left them natural. If you cut these pieces from pine or other light wood, stain them dark.

ASSEMBLE & SHAPE THE NECK

Cut saw slots for frets in the fingerboard according to the spacing shown in the pattern opposite, then widen the slots with a triangular file.

Fasten the fingerboard to the neck with glue and brads.

Using a rasp or electric sander loaded with coarse paper, sand the fingerboard and neck until they blend together. For authenticity, you can shape the peghead so it is thinner than the neck and slopes back from it, as shown at top.

Angle the nest box to fit between the blocks, in the lower curve of the guitar back.

BUILD & INSTALL THE NEST BOX

Glue, then nail the neck and tail blocks in position on the back.

Build the nest box and angle it to fit between the blocks so that it sits within the lower curve of the guitar back, as shown above.

Trace around the inside of the nest box with a pencil, then cut an opening in the back ¾ inch narrower on each side to allow a surface for fastening the box.

Fasten the back to the nest box with glue and nails. ➤

FRONT, BACK & BRIDGE PATTERN

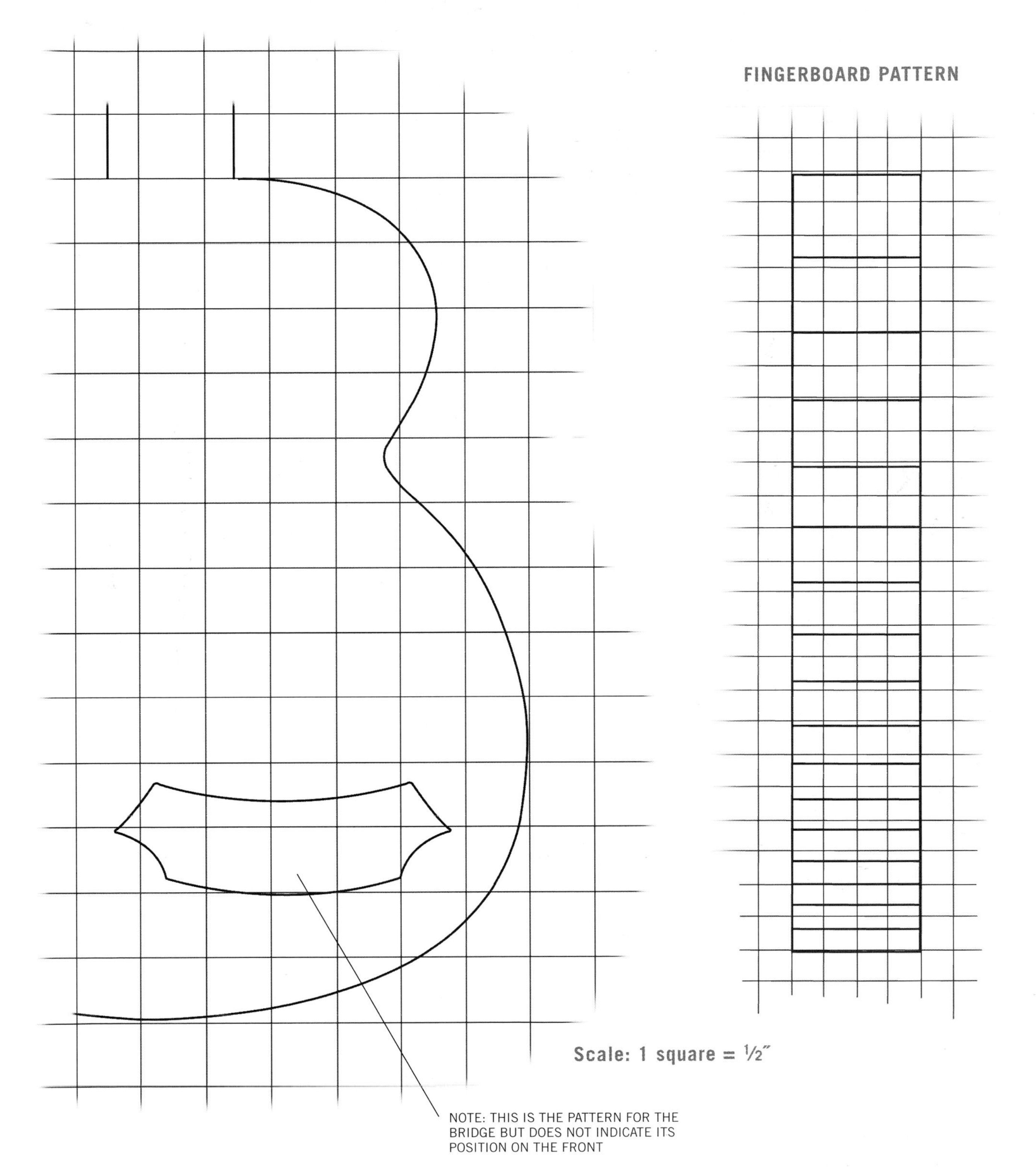

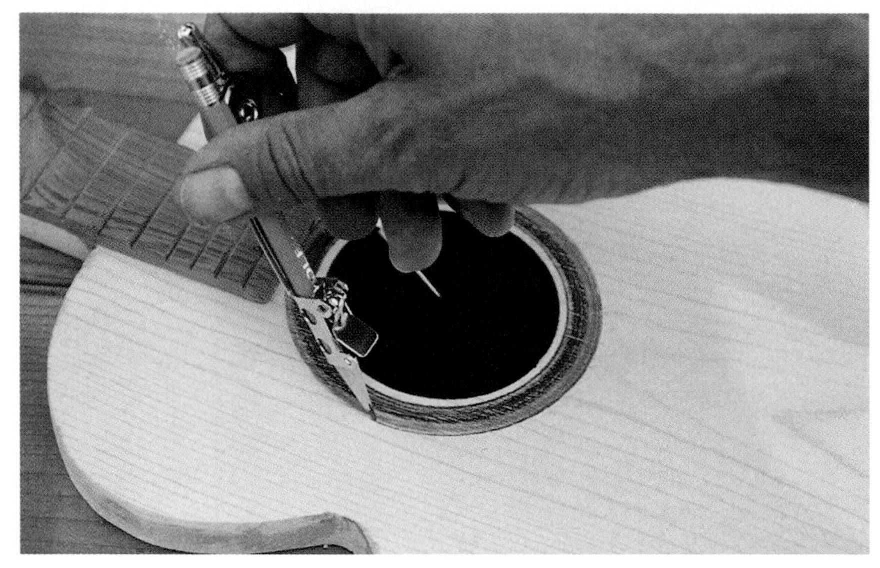

Use a compass and pencil to make concentric circles around the sound-hole rosette, then color.

FINISH THE FRONT

Mask off the area of the entry hole and the sound-hole rosette. Mark the center point for the hole and, using a compass, mark a 3-inch circle around it. Attach a razor knife to the compass and cut out the circle.

Remove the masking tape within the circle and paint the area flat black. Remove the rest of the tape and make a sound-hole rosette by using a compass and pencil to make concentric circles, then coloring each circle a different shade, as shown above.

Finally, drill the entry hole and paint its inner edges flat black. Spray the entire front with misting coats of clear gloss polyurethane.

PREPARE THE REMAINING PARTS

Cut 5 feet of flashing and drill 1⁄16-inch holes 3⁄8 inch in from each edge, 2 inches apart.

Sand and paint all flashing and the guitar back with the rust-color primer. Paint the saddle, nut, and bridge pins white and the tuning pegs gold. Stain the neck and peghead a dark color.

Make "tuners" from scrap wood and thumbscrews, and paint gold.

ASSEMBLE THE BODY

Place the front on the back/nest box assembly. Cut a notch at one end of the flashing to clear half the neck, then bend the flashing around the body and nail it to the front and back with 5⁄8-inch brads. Trim the flashing so it is flush with the front and clears the neck.

Drill holes in the neck block and nail the flashing edges to it. Drill a pair of 5⁄8-inch drain holes through the lower right corner of the side and through the nesting-box floor.

ADD THE DETAILS & FINAL FINISH

Cut frets from the brass rod and attach to the grooves in the neck with silicone. Fasten the bridge to the front with glue and brads driven into 3⁄16-inch holes 1⁄2 inch deep in the bridge. Glue the saddle to the bridge and the nut to the neck. Drill 1⁄4-inch holes in the peghead and tap in the tuning pegs.

Glue the tuners in position and secure each with a brad.

Touch-up the paint and spray the entire project with gloss polyurethane.

STRING IT UP!

When fully dry, trim the body with vinyl tape. If you stretch the tape as you go, it will naturally bend over the front, creating a top binding.

Fasten the tape at the guitar's waist with brads and cut away about an inch at the waist so the piece is flush with the top. "Fill in" this binding with a black permanent marker.

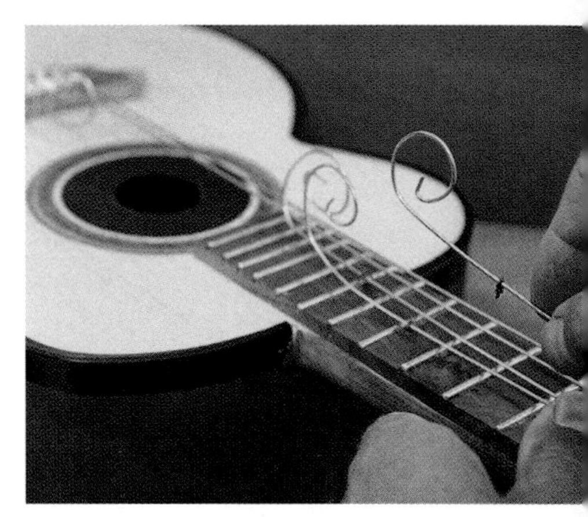

Artfully curl back three or four strings from the "sound hole" to allow for entry of birds.

Finally, add strings made of copper wire by pinning one end with a bridge pin driven gently into the holes in the bridge and wrapping the other end around a tuning peg.

Cut the inner three or four strings where they run across the entry hole and curl them back into artful spirals, as shown above. Fasten these strings to the fingerboard with light-gauge steel wire twisted over the strings and driven into 3⁄16-inch holes.

Hang your musical birdhouse from its strap and wait for the rockin' robins to thank you with their songs.

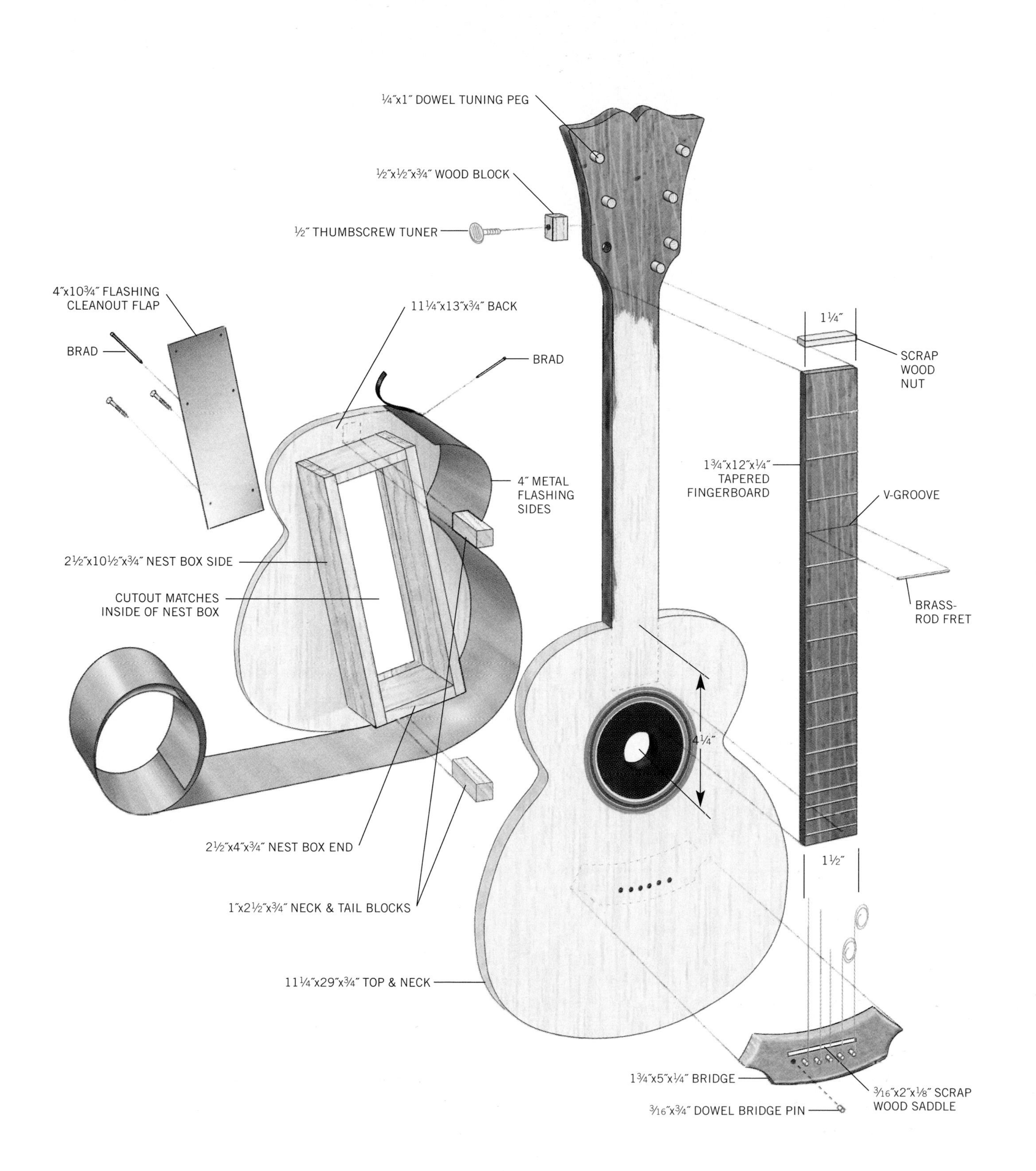
¼″x1″ DOWEL TUNING PEG
½″x½″x¾″ WOOD BLOCK
½″ THUMBSCREW TUNER
4″x10¾″ FLASHING
CLEANOUT FLAP
11¼″x13″x¾″ BACK
BRAD
BRAD
1¼″
SCRAP
WOOD
NUT
4″ METAL
FLASHING
SIDES
1¾″x12″x¼″
TAPERED
FINGERBOARD
V-GROOVE
2½″x10½″x¾″ NEST BOX SIDE
CUTOUT MATCHES
INSIDE OF NEST BOX
BRASS-
ROD FRET
4¼″
2½″x4″x¾″ NEST BOX END
1½″
1″x2½″x¾″ NECK & TAIL BLOCKS
11¼″x29″x¾″ TOP & NECK
1¾″x5″x¼″ BRIDGE
3⁄16″x2″x⅛″ SCRAP
WOOD SADDLE
3⁄16″x¾″ DOWEL BRIDGE PIN

Cliff Dwelling

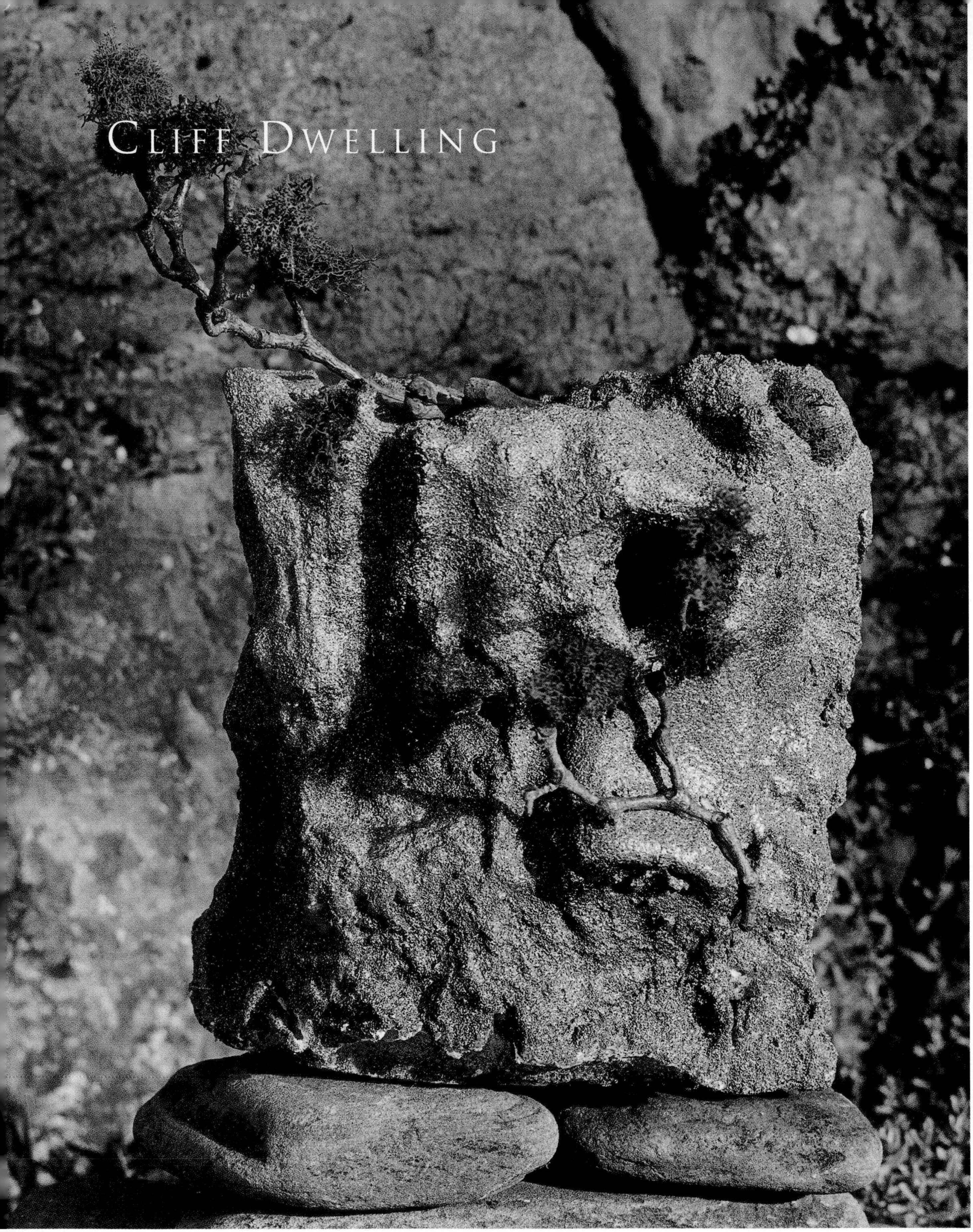

This project is more like model-making than classic birdhouse building, but a birdhouse it is, none-theless. When friends ask how you did it, you can tell them it's simply made of fiber-reinforced polymerized plaster over a sacrificial base (only you need to know that it's just patching plaster on cheesecloth laid over a rigid foam-cov-ered cardboard box).

The interior structure provides sup-port for the plaster-and-cheesecloth shell, plus insulation for the birds. The cliff dwelling is weatherized enough to stand up to an occasional shower, but don't leave it outside all year long.

It's perfect as a collector's bird-house, in which case you might want to elaborate on the scale-model elements. How about a live bonsai tree?

MATERIALS

- ¾-inch plywood: 1 square foot
- Corrugated cardboard
- Rigid foam scraps
- Hot-melt glue
- 1¼-inch drywall screws: 3
- Cheesecloth: about 10 square feet
- Plaster patching compound: about 3 pounds
- Trimmings: twigs, driftwood, artificial moss, etc.
- Spray paint: rust-color primer, flat black, faux granite finish
- Spray polyurethane exterior finish: clear satin

TOOLS

- Basic hand tools
- Jigsaw, coping saw, band saw, or scroll saw
- Electric drill, bits, and 3-inch hole saw
- Staple gun
- Propane torch
- Disposable latex gloves

MAKE THE BOX

Cut the multifaceted shape shown in the illustration on page 97 from the plywood. Then cut a 3-inch circular opening in the center of the base for mounting and cleanout.

Hot-glue and staple 10-inch-long corrugated cardboard panels to the edges of the base, as shown at right. Overlap the panels and hot-glue them to each other. Cut the panel tops in straight lines, but at odd angles to each other, to create an irregular plane for the box top.

Cut and add the top, gluing it to the sides, as shown in the illustration on page 97.

ADD THE RIGID FOAM

Break up rigid foam packing blocks and hot-glue randomly to the cardboard. The high-density material from ship-ping cartons works best, but you can also get lower-density rigid foam at hobby shops and crafts stores. Butt blocks of foam together, as shown at right, to create a highly uneven sur-face—the rougher the better.

Working outdoors with a propane torch, melt the foam so that when its surface hardens it forms "tortured" shapes, as shown at bottom right. Take care not to light it on fire, and stay upwind as you work.

Melt an entry hole in the foam, then cut through the cardboard with a utility knife. ➤

Using hot glue and staples, attach the corru-gated cardboard panels to the plywood base.

Break up foam blocks and butt them together to create a highly uneven surface.

Melt the foam using a propane torch so that when it hardens it forms "tortured" shapes.

Spray-paint the surface rust, then flat black, and finish with faux-stone.

"Trees" made from snaggly twigs and moss complete the house.

ADD THE PLASTER

Fold the cheesecloth double or triple thick and cut into manageable pieces a foot or so square. Mix two cups of plaster patching compound with water until it's the consistency of thick pancake batter.

Wearing gloves, immerse a square of cheesecloth in the plaster, then apply it to the box. Add additional plaster with your hands, pressing the cloth firmly onto the box. Continue with additional batches until the box is fully covered (don't forget to coat the sides of the entry hole as well) and the plaster is about a quarter-inch thick. Allow it to cure overnight.

PAINT THE "ROCK"

Spray-paint the entire surface of the "rock" with the rust color. Follow with flat black, but leave the rust color on the higher spots. Finish with faux-stone spray finish, as shown top left, but allow the rust to show through here and there and some of the black to remain in the hollows and crevices.

Let dry overnight, then topcoat with several coats of satin polyurethane (exterior or interior, depending on the project's final location).

ADD THE TRIMMINGS

Make a tree or two from snaggly twigs and artificial moss. Add driftwood logs, moss bushes, and anything else you like, using hot glue to affix, as shown above right.

If the house will be exposed to rain, use waterproof wood glue instead, and spray-finish your trimmings with clear satin polyurethane.

Attach the floor hatch to its supports with the screws, unless you're post-mounting, in which case, follow the instructions for the Seashell Sand Castle on page 78.

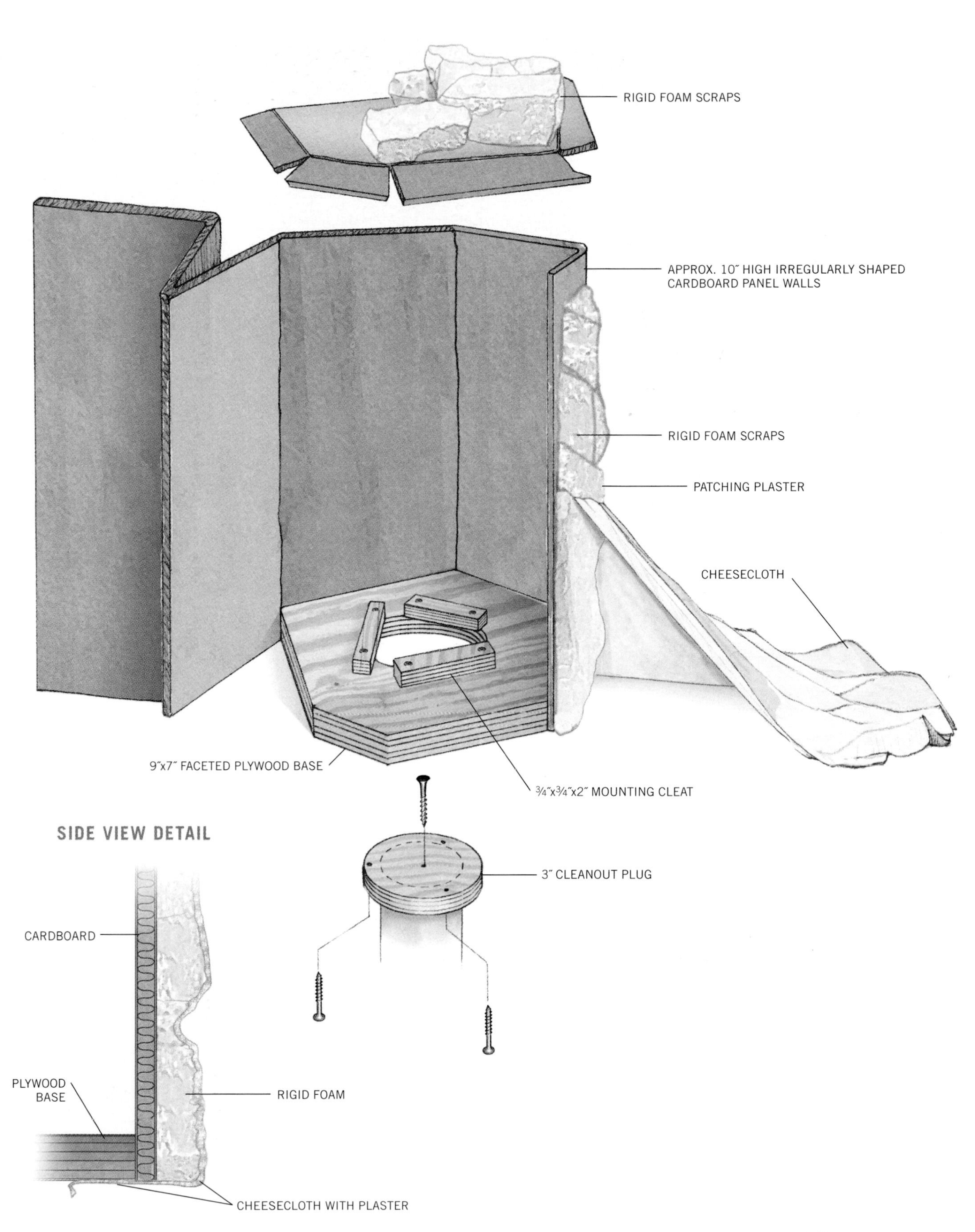
RIGID FOAM SCRAPS
APPROX. 10″ HIGH IRREGULARLY SHAPED CARDBOARD PANEL WALLS
RIGID FOAM SCRAPS
PATCHING PLASTER
CHEESECLOTH
9″x7″ FACETED PLYWOOD BASE
¾″x¾″x2″ MOUNTING CLEAT
SIDE VIEW DETAIL
3″ CLEANOUT PLUG
CARDBOARD
PLYWOOD BASE
RIGID FOAM
CHEESECLOTH WITH PLASTER

Noah's Ark

Unlike its 40-day prototype, our solid-wood ark is designed for only one couple at a time.

Construction is direct and simple. Wood stacks are sandwiched between upper and lower football shapes, then roughed out with a saw and rasp and finished with a sander. It's carving made simple.

The house at the center of the hull has the same dimensions as our Basic Birdhouse (see page 43), designed for the widest possible range of species and easily adapted for others.

We've trimmed our ark simply, however, this sturdy little boat is a virtual blank canvas for fancy paint jobs, portholes, animals (carved or plastic), and, of course, a dove on the roof.

PREPARE THE PARTS

Enlarge the pattern on page 100 by 400 percent and trace each football onto the redwood or cedar 1 by 8. Cut out these and all other parts. Glue and nail the house walls together, and mark and drill an entry hole according to the chart on page 126.

Center the house on the top football-shaped piece and trace its outline, then repeat on the bottom piece. Measure ¾ inch in from the two side wall lines on the bottom piece and then draw in those cutting lines.

With a jigsaw, coping saw, or scroll saw, cut the openings in the footballs. Retain the cutout scrap from the bottom one to serve as a cleanout plug.

Glue and nail (from below) the house sides to the lower football. Attach the cleanout plug to the gable ends of the house with outdoor screws.

ASSEMBLE THE STACKS

To make the hull stacks, cut 1-by-8 stock so that the grain runs fore and aft. For the bottom piece in each stack, allow a ½- to ¾-inch overlap of the bottom football. Make each succeeding piece ½ to ¾ inch longer than the one beneath it.

Glue and screw the stacks together using six 2-inch drywall screws, three from above and three from below. Butt the stacks firmly against the house's gable walls and screw through the bottom football. Glue and nail the top football in place. Glue and nail the side pieces in place, countersinking the nails deeply. ➤

MATERIALS

- 1-by-8 redwood or cedar: 7 feet
- 1-by-4 redwood or cedar: 2 feet
- 1-by-6 pine or other softwood: 3 feet
- ¼-inch plywood: 1 square foot
- Cedar shingle shims: 1 bundle
- 3d galvanized finishing nails
- ½-inch brads
- Bronze upholstery nails
- 1-inch drywall screws: 4
- 2-inch drywall screws: 12
- 1½-inch outdoor screws: 2
- Exterior wood glue
- ¼-inch-by-2-inch bolt, nut, and two washers: 1
- Redwood or cedar wood filler
- Coarse and fine sandpaper
- Oil-based stain: dark color
- Transparent deck finish

TOOLS

- Basic hand tools
- Jigsaw, coping saw, or scroll saw
- Electric drill, bits, and spade bit or hole saw for entry hole
- Belt sander or coarse sanding disk for electric drill

OPTIONAL: Reciprocating saw or small chainsaw

Sandwich the hull stacks between the footballs, glue and nail together, then affix the side pieces.

With a sander or sanding attachment, rough out the hull shape, working across the grain.

After finish-sanding the ark with fine sandpaper, dust thoroughly and apply the finish.

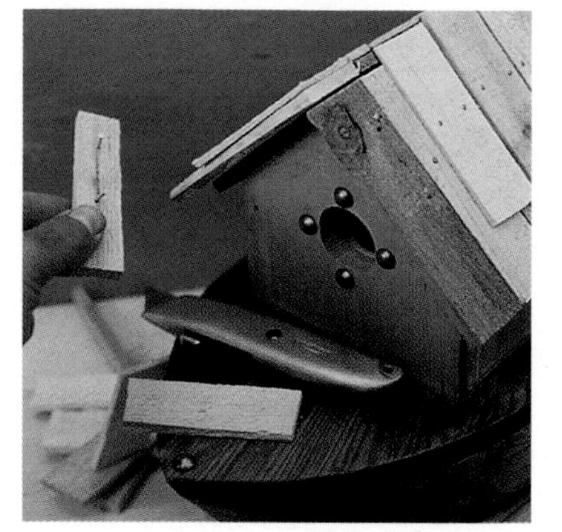

Attach the shingles so that the nails in the lower rows are covered by the shingles above.

SHAPE THE HULL

Bolt a foot-long scrap of 1 by 4 or 2 by 4 to the center of the entry hole. Use the projecting end to mount the hull assembly upside down in a vise.

Remove the exposed screws and with a handsaw cut the projecting corners off the stacks.

Next, rough out the hull shape with a rasp (or reciprocating saw or small chainsaw). Finish the shape using a sander with a coarse belt, as shown at top left, or use a coarse sanding disk mounted in an electric drill, working across the grain and beveling the footballs, stacks, and side pieces.

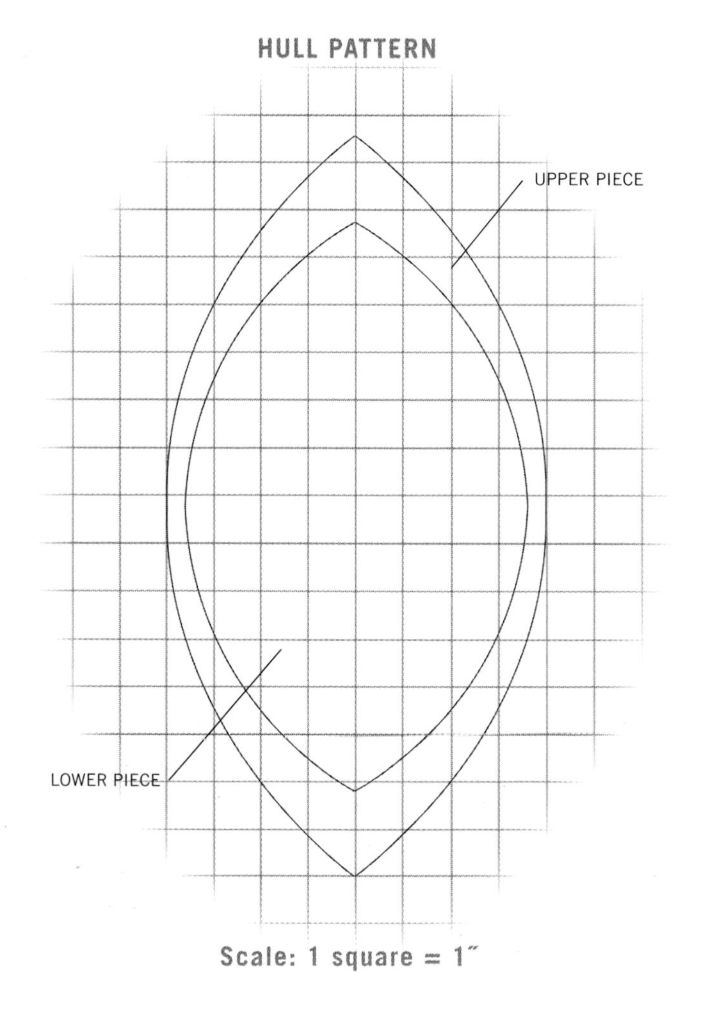

FINISH THE HULL

Demount the hull and bore the entry hole to size. Countersink the nails and fill the nail holes and any chinks in the hull with wood filler.

Using a handsaw, scribe lines across the hull side pieces so they match up with the lines between the fore and aft stacks. Finish-sand the ark with fine sandpaper. Dust thoroughly and apply transparent deck finish to all exterior surfaces, as shown at middle top.

SHINGLE THE ROOF

Add the upholstery nails to the house and hull.

Stain the underside and edges of the roof pieces a dark color, then attach them with 3d nails.

Cut shingles from the cedar shims to fit as shown above. For the best appearance, cut 3 or 4 inches off the thick end of the shims and work with the remainder.

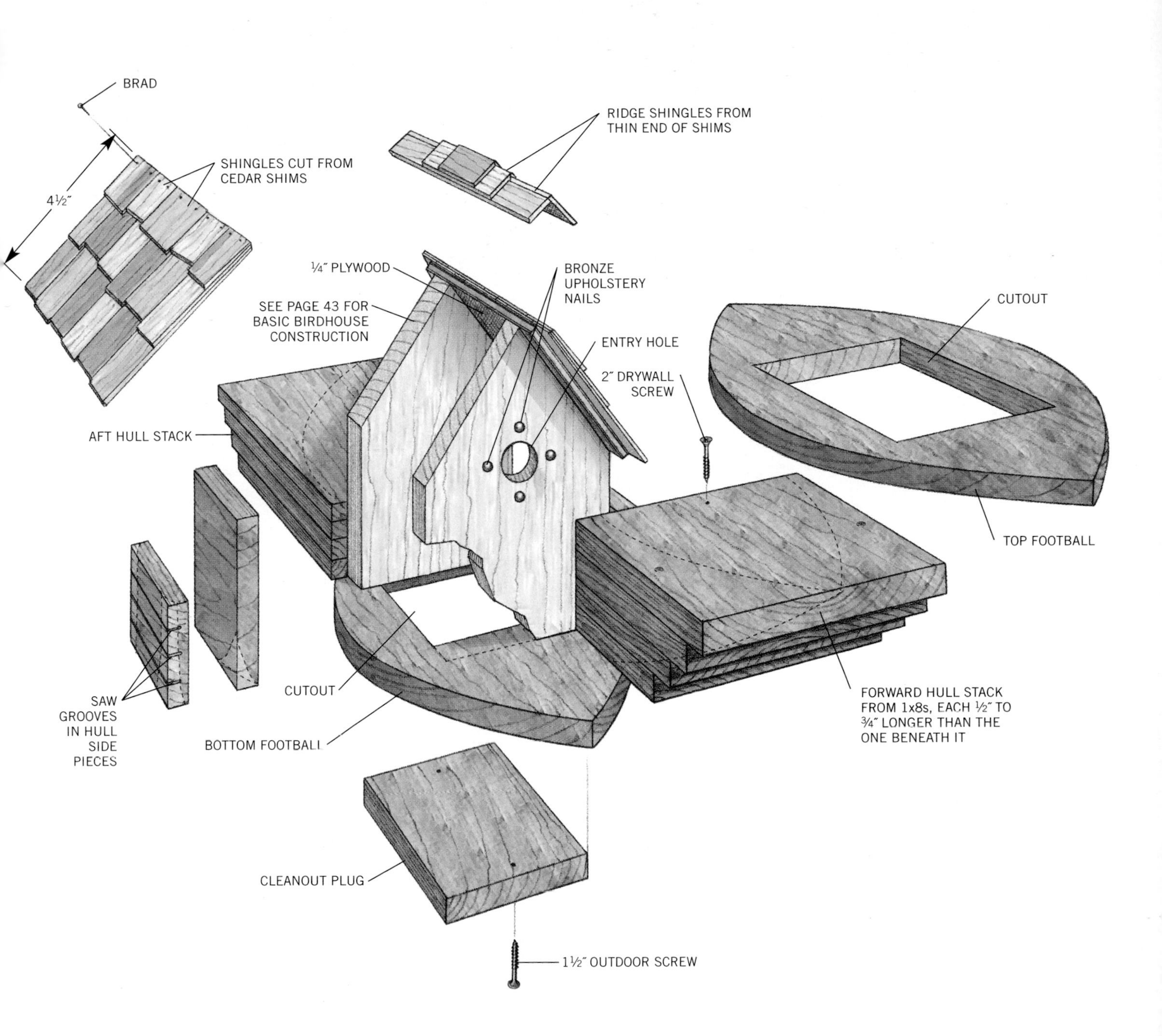

Cut the lower-most shingles to run from the ridge to about ⅜ inch beyond the eaves. The middle row should run about two-thirds of the way down from the ridge, the top row about a third of the way down, and both should vary in length and width. All the shingles that overhang the gable ends should do so by about ⅝ inch.

Attach the shingles with brads so that the nails in the lower rows are covered by the shingles above. Nip ⅛ inch from the tips of the brads or 3d nails used to attach the gable-end shingles so the nails don't go through the plywood.

Split the ridge shingles from the thin end of the shims and attach them with nails, or if you don't want any nails showing, use glue to fasten them to the surface.

GAZEBO BIRDFEEDER

This stylish feeder will lend a touch of 19th-century grace to any garden—and stand up to the elements, too. The design is decorative enough to make the feeder a focal point in your yard, and it's fun to watch birds come and go. A high-rimmed tray helps contain the seed, and narrowish openings discourage squirrels.

This "fancy" variation of the one shown on the cover includes moldings, an antiqued finish, and a copper roof, but is just as simple to build. Be sure you place it in a shaded area since the copper will heat up quickly in the sun.

LAY OUT & CUT THE PARTS

Lay out and cut the three hexagons, as shown in the illustrations on page 105. Then drill a ⅛-inch hole in the center of each hexagon.

Make a pattern for a single roof panel from cardboard. Mark the layout of the roof on the underside of the sheet metal, as shown in the diagram on page 105.

Crosscut 12 pieces of ¾-inch lattice to 6½ inches each.

ASSEMBLE THE BASIC PARTS

Attach the base hexagon to the floor hexagon with glue, using a nail through the center holes to help align the sides, then drive in three 1¼-inch screws from beneath. Affix the 1-inch dowel in the center of the ceiling hexagon with glue and a 2-inch screw.

Next, with glue and brads, connect the two hexagonal parts with the 12 lattice pieces by fastening a pair butted together at each of the six corners. Cut the top and bottom infill pieces from the 1½-inch lattice (measure for each one since there are apt to be slight irregularities). With a coping saw or scroll saw, trim the upper infill pieces to form a decorative curve, then fasten the pieces with glue and brads.

ADD THE TRIM

Cut pieces of 1-inch decorative molding to run around the bottom and top of the feeder. If your molding has a running pattern, cut the pieces in succession so that the pattern will be continuous. Bevel the ends of each piece at 30 degrees with an electric sander or sanding block. Fasten with glue and brads, as shown above right. (You needn't be perfect in this work; in fact, a little roughness is part of the charm.)

After all the bottom moldings are in place, cut six pieces of 5⁄16-inch-diameter dowel 4 inches long and glue them in the open joints between the uprights, atop the bottom row of trim moldings. Finish with another row of molding pieces at the top, supported by the dowels. ➤

Decorative molding, attached top and bottom, is an easy way to dress up your feeder.

MATERIALS

- 1-by-8 pine or other softwood: 1 foot
- 1-by-6 pine or other softwood: 1 foot
- ¼-inch-by-¾-inch lattice: 5 feet
- ¼-inch-by-1½-inch lattice: 2 feet
- 5⁄16-inch dowel: 3 feet
- ¼-inch-by-1-inch decorative molding: 5 feet
- 1-inch dowel: 6 inches
- Wooden cabinet knob or finial
- Lightweight copper: 16 inches square
- 1-inch brads
- 1-inch outdoor screws: 3
- 2-inch outdoor screw: 1
- Exterior wood glue
- Fine sandpaper
- Water- or oil-based primer & paint
- Metal patina finish
- Spray polyurethane exterior finish: clear satin

OPTIONAL: 1½-inch copper pipe cap; three 1¼-inch outdoor screws or drywall screws

TOOLS

- Basic hand tools
- Jigsaw, coping saw, band saw, or scroll saw
- Electric drill and bits

OPTIONAL: Table saw, electric sander

For an antiqued finish, dab thinned oil-based paint on the surface and wipe with a sponge.

When bending and shaping the roof, use a scrap block to cushion the hammer blows.

The dowel will need to be trimmed slightly so that the roof can be hammered over it.

APPLY THE PAINT

Paint the entire structure, plus the cabinet knob or wood finial, with flat white, oil-based primer. Allow to dry.

Create the wiped finish by dabbing thinned, water-based paint over the entire surface, then wiping it off with a sponge, as shown above. (We created the ivy-green color used by mixing blue, yellow, and black tempera cut 50 percent with faux glazing liquid to ensure good flow and plenty of working time before drying.)

When the paint is dry, lightly dab highlights with a brush barely dipped in white paint. Allow to dry, then topcoat with satin polyurethane.

BEND & SHAPE THE ROOF

Lay a metal straightedge on the first roof-segment line on the sheet metal and fold the metal all the way over. Hammer it nearly flat, using a piece of scrap wood to cushion the blows, as shown at middle top. This creates a soft crease along the ridgeline-to-be.

Next, placing your fingers on either side of the fold, unbend the panel until it leaves a "standing seam" about a half-inch high. Repeat with the other panels, including the half-panel.

Finally, shape the entire roof piece into a cone, with the half-panel overlapping the first panel.

FASTEN THE ROOF IN PLACE

Place the roof in position, form the bottom around the ceiling hexagon, and press the top in against the dowel. Trim the dowel so that the top ¼ inch or so of the roof can be hammered over on top of it, as shown at top right, then fasten with two or three brads.

Fasten the lower edge of the roof to the ceiling hexagon with a brad at the center of each panel.

Finally, drill a pilot hole in the center of the dowel and screw on the cabinet knob or finial. (If you're using a cabinet knob, drive its mounting screw in halfway, cut off the head, then screw on the knob.)

FINISH THE ROOF

A number of creative and fun patina finishes are on the market these days. To achieve the look shown here, we scrubbed the copper roof with copper cleanser, rinsed and dried it, then applied two coats of blue patina finish. When this was dry, we rubbed it gently under running water with a sponge until we had the look we wanted. A coat of polyurethane will help the patina adhere.

POLE-MOUNT THE FEEDER

To mount the feeder, we used a copper pipe cap sized to the diameter of our pole, attached to the feeder base with three 1-inch screws. The pipe cap/feeder assembly was then secured by a screw driven through the side of the pipe cap into the pole.

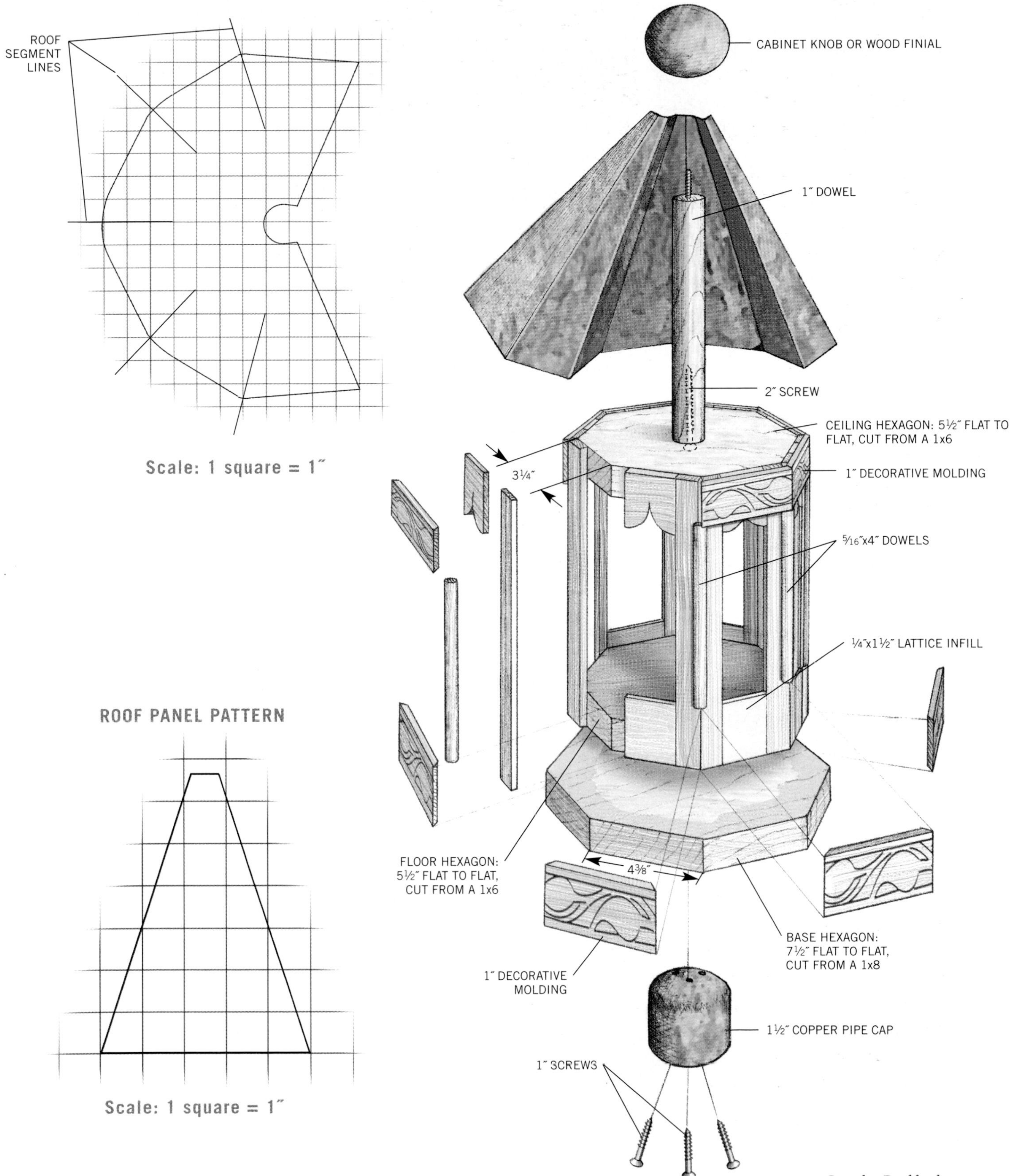
ROOF PATTERN
ROOF
SEGMENT
LINES
Scale: 1 square = 1″
ROOF PANEL PATTERN
Scale: 1 square = 1″
CABINET KNOB OR WOOD FINIAL
1″ DOWEL
2″ SCREW
CEILING HEXAGON: 5½″ FLAT TO
FLAT, CUT FROM A 1x6
1″ DECORATIVE MOLDING
3¼″
5⁄16″x4″ DOWELS
¼″x1½″ LATTICE INFILL
FLOOR HEXAGON:
5½″ FLAT TO FLAT,
CUT FROM A 1x6
4⅜″
BASE HEXAGON:
7½″ FLAT TO FLAT,
CUT FROM A 1x8
1″ DECORATIVE
MOLDING
1½″ COPPER PIPE CAP
1″ SCREWS

Old Cape Lighthouse

Lighthouses have an almost mystical appeal—in this case, a glowing lantern atop a boldly striped tower provides safety for skyfarers.

As a practical matter, building a lighthouse's requisite tapered octagon can be a real challenge, even for an experienced woodworker. We've designed ours to be easy and forgiving, however, and you can put it together in an afternoon with just basic tools.

The lighthouse is fully weatherproofed for use outdoors, but it's also at home indoors as a decorative piece—or even a fine lamp base.

PREPARE THE PARTS

Cut out the octagons A, B, and C, plus the plywood staves to the dimensions shown in the diagrams on pages 108 and 109.

Drill the entry hole in one stave. Drill ¼-inch holes in the centers of octagons A and B and a 3-inch hole in the center of octagon C.

For the base, cut any irregular shape you like from about 8 inches of the 1 by 8; just be sure that octagon C will fit in it with at least ½-inch clearance all around. Cut a 4-inch hole in the base and save the cut-out piece for the cleanout plug.

To make the lantern parts, cut the top half-inch or so from the PVC pipe cap (a miter box is helpful) and drill a ¼-inch hole in its center. Cut out a 3-inch disk from the plywood, and drill a ¼-inch hole in its center. Paint the PVC coupling yellow.

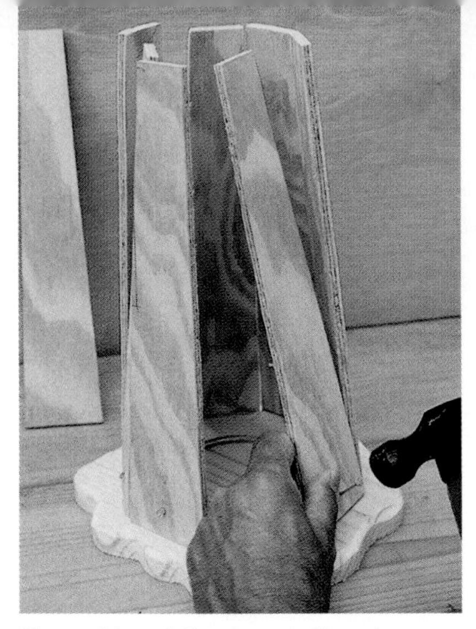

Glue and toenail the staves to the octagon facets after octagon C is affixed to the base.

Plaster between the staves and the base, the base surface, and the scrap wood.

Mask the tower and lantern, spray with black paint, allow to dry, then remove the masking.

ASSEMBLE THE DECK

Stack octagons A and octagon B as shown in the illustration on page 109. To align them, run the toggle bolt through their holes but don't fasten it.

Rotate the pieces to align their edges, then glue and screw the parts together, running in 1½-inch screws from below.

BUILD THE TOWER

Fasten octagon C to the base with glue and brads.

Glue and toenail the staves to the octagon facets, using a single 3d box nail for each, as shown above. Drop in the deck assembly and glue the top edge of each stave to the lower plywood octagon A, then fasten with 1-inch drywall screws.

When the glue is dry, sand all the surfaces smooth. Fasten the cleanout plug in place with the two remaining drywall screws.

PLASTER THE BASE & TOWER

Fill in around the base of the tower with broken scraps of 1 by, then glue them in place.

Mix patching plaster to the consistency of very thick pancake batter. With a putty knife, fill the open joints between the staves. Wearing rubber gloves, fill the joint between the staves and the base with your fingers. Finally, plaster over the base and scrap wood, as shown above.

To get a nice breaking-wave effect, use the putty knife to press globs of plaster into the angle of the base and staves; press inward and draw the knife downward and the plaster will flow over the top of the knife, creating a wavelike curl.

MASK & PAINT

When the plaster has set, sand the stave joints and base fillet smooth, then paint the entire assembly, plus the lantern cap and disk, with a coat of flat white primer.

Attach the lantern parts to the deck with the toggle bolt, making sure the PVC coupling is centered on the deck and under the cap assembly.

Mask the lantern and tower as shown at top right. To mask the base, cut a 4-inch slit in the bottom of a plastic bag and slide the bag over the lantern and tower until it overlaps the lowest piece of masking tape. The ➤

MATERIALS

- 1-by-8 pine or other softwood or ¾-inch plywood: 2 feet
- ¼-inch plywood: about 1 square foot
- ¼-dowel: 2 inches
- 1½-inch PVC pipe cap
- 2-inch PVC coupling
- 3d galvanized box nails
- ⅝-inch brads
- #6-by-1-inch drywall screws: 8
- #6-by-1½-inch drywall screws: 2
- 6-by-¼-inch toggle bolt: 1
- Exterior wood glue
- Plaster patching compound: 2 cups (dry)
- Spray enamel: flat white primer, yellow, flat black
- Tempera paints: yellow, blue, white
- Spray polyurethane exterior finish: clear satin

TOOLS

- Basic hand tools
- Jigsaw, coping saw, band saw, or scroll saw
- Electric drill, bits, and spade bit or hole saw for entry hole

OPTIONAL: Table saw, miter box, electric sander

Mix yellow and blue, then stipple on to create waves in shades of blues and greens.

opening will expand and cling tightly to the tower as you do so. Secure the bag with masking tape.

Spray the lantern and tower with several coats of flat black. Let the paint dry, and remove the masking.

MAKE WAVES

Place a couple of tablespoons each of the three tempera colors side-by-side in a plastic cup but don't mix them. Dip a stiff brush in water, then dip it in the intersection of the blue and yellow paints. Draw the brush up the side of the cup and mix there until you get a nice sea-green. Then stipple this color all around the base of the tower, as shown above.

Continue in this manner, mixing variegated blues and greens and shading to a lighter green as you approach the tops of the waves. Let these colors dry (it only takes a few minutes), then cap off your "surf" with white at the tops of the waves.

Allow to dry thoroughly, then spray with several coats of polyurethane.

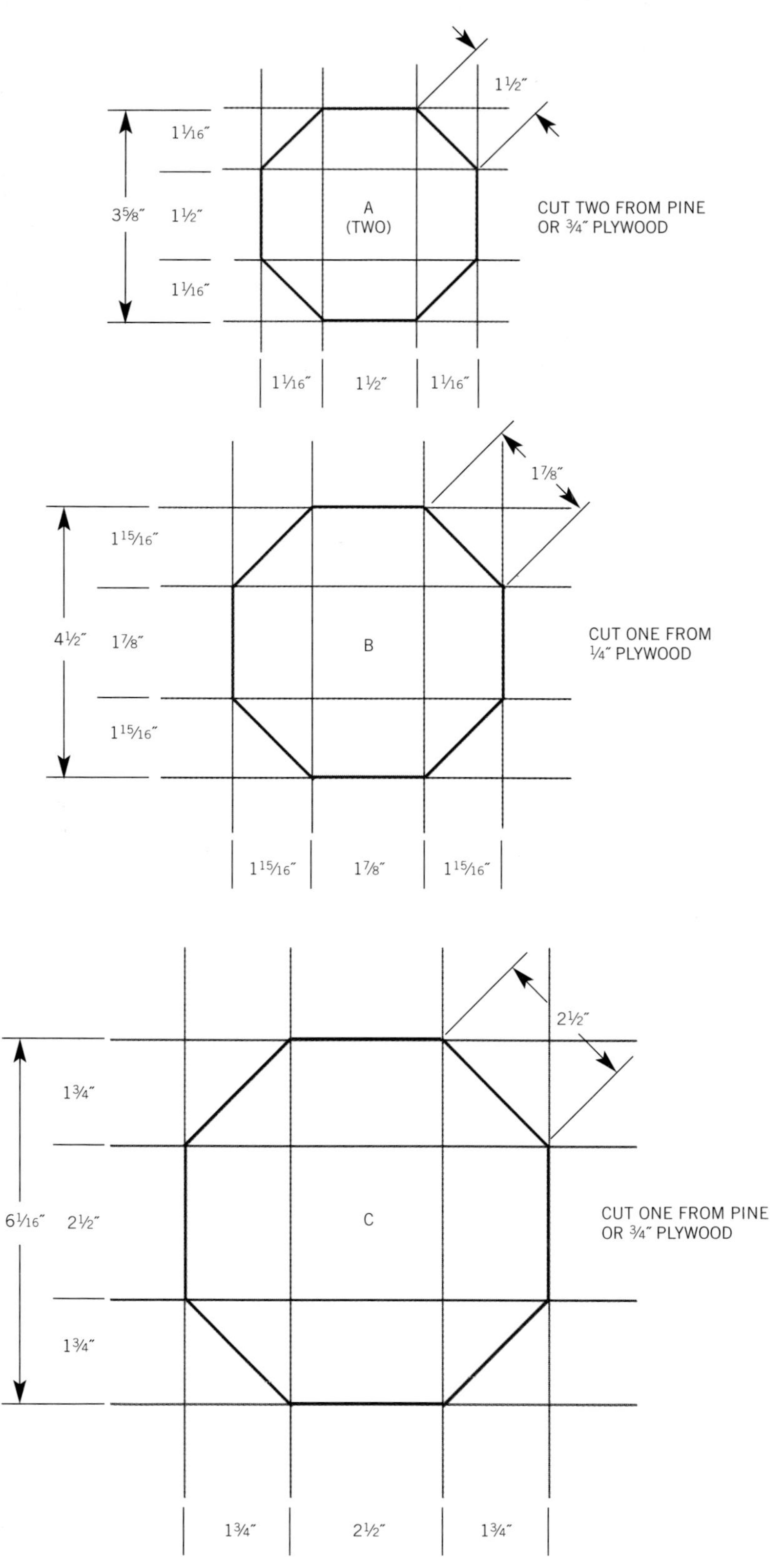

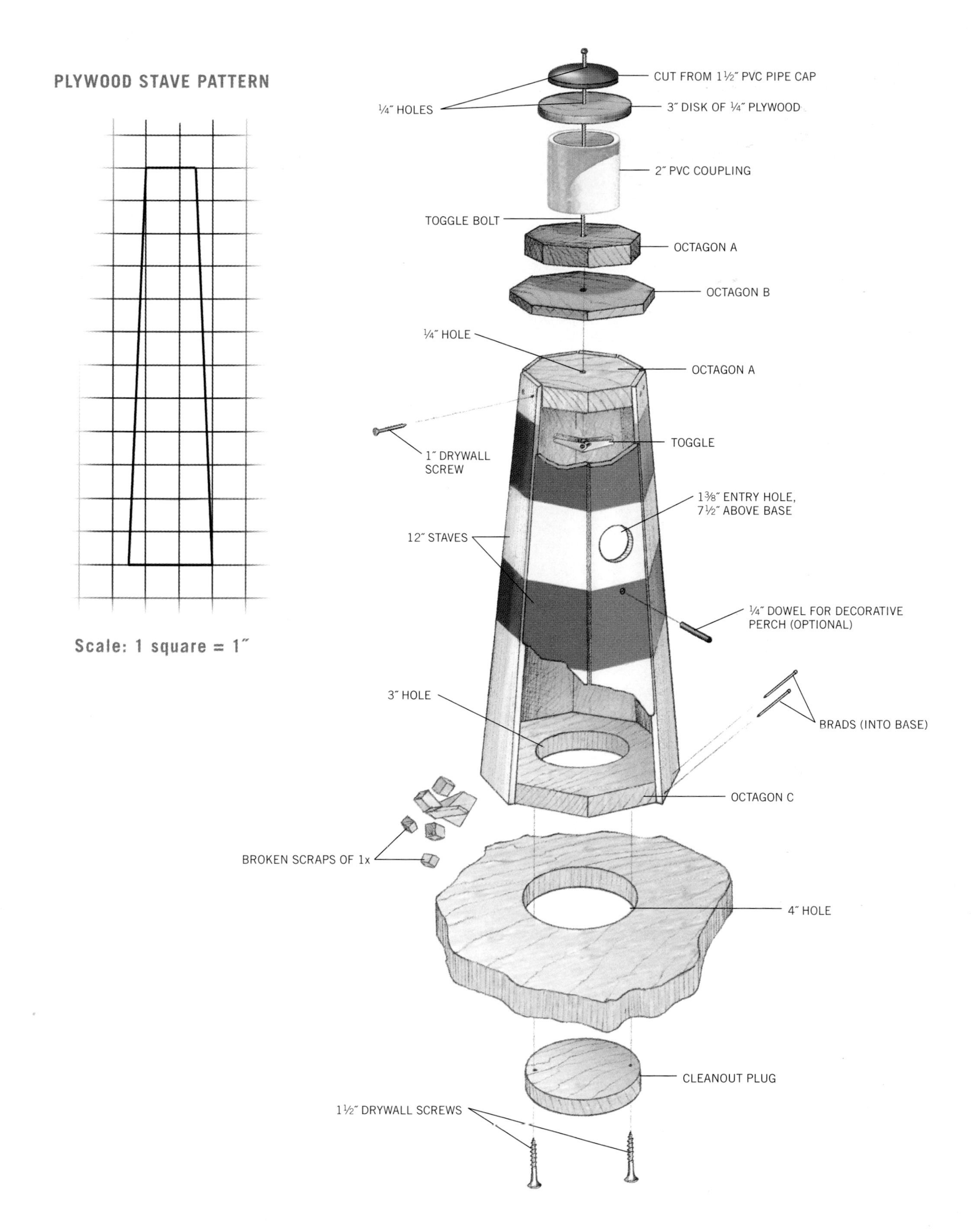
PLYWOOD STAVE PATTERN
Scale: 1 square = 1″
CUT FROM 1½″ PVC PIPE CAP
¼″ HOLES
3″ DISK OF ¼″ PLYWOOD
2″ PVC COUPLING
TOGGLE BOLT
OCTAGON A
OCTAGON B
¼″ HOLE
OCTAGON A
TOGGLE
1″ DRYWALL SCREW
1⅜″ ENTRY HOLE, 7½″ ABOVE BASE
12″ STAVES
¼″ DOWEL FOR DECORATIVE PERCH (OPTIONAL)
3″ HOLE
BRADS (INTO BASE)
OCTAGON C
BROKEN SCRAPS OF 1x
4″ HOLE
CLEANOUT PLUG
1½″ DRYWALL SCREWS

ROUTE 66

Cruising down the highway with the wind blowing through their hair, our retro couple is the epitome of fifties bliss.

A perfect decorative accessory for a rec room, this whimsical birdhouse is also a practical nesting-season home for smaller species (see pages 126–127).

The project is extremely simple to build. We've provided the professional graphics, so there's no artistic ability required. All you need to do is cut out the parts, assemble them, and paste on the artwork.

PREPARE THE GRAPHICS

Make one black-and-white copy and one high-quality color copy each of the car and trailer patterns on page 114. Use heavy paper and copy both of them at actual size.

Spray the color copies with satin polyurethane finish on both sides and set aside. Trim the black-and-white car and trailer patterns to within an inch or so of the outline; then, with spray adhesive or rubber cement, mount it to a 1-by-8 board.

CUT OUT THE PARTS

With a coping saw, jigsaw, or scroll saw, cut out the car and trailer along the pattern lines, as shown below, bypassing any areas the blade won't easily reach. When you've finished cutting out the basic shapes, you'll be able to easily cut directly into these areas. File and sand the edges, if necessary, to achieve a close fit to the patterns.

Bore the entry hole (it can be anywhere from 1 inch to 1⅜ inch in diameter, depending on the type of bird you want to attract). Drill a ⅛-inch pilot hole in the rear wall directly opposite the center of the entry hole.

On the remainder of the 1 by 8, trace around the trailer wall and cut out to make the rear wall.

Paint the edges of the car and trailer flat black.

Cut the rear ¾-inch support cleat from scrap 1 by 8. Cut the floor from ¼-inch plywood.

Drill a 1⁄16-inch hole in the center of each screw-hole button. Paint the buttons red for the tail lights. ➤

MATERIALS

- 1-by-8 pine or other softwood: 3 feet
- ¼-inch plywood: about 1 square foot
- 6-inch aluminum flashing: 2 feet
- ½-inch brads
- #6-by-1-inch drywall screws: 8
- Exterior wood glue
- ⅜-inch screw-hole buttons: 2
- Spray adhesive or rubber cement
- Fine sandpaper
- Spray enamel: flat black
- Black permanent marker
- Spray polyurethane exterior finish: clear satin

TOOLS

- Basic hand tools
- Jigsaw, coping saw, band saw, or scroll saw
- Electric drill, bits, and spade bit or hole saw for entry hole

OPTIONAL: Electric sander

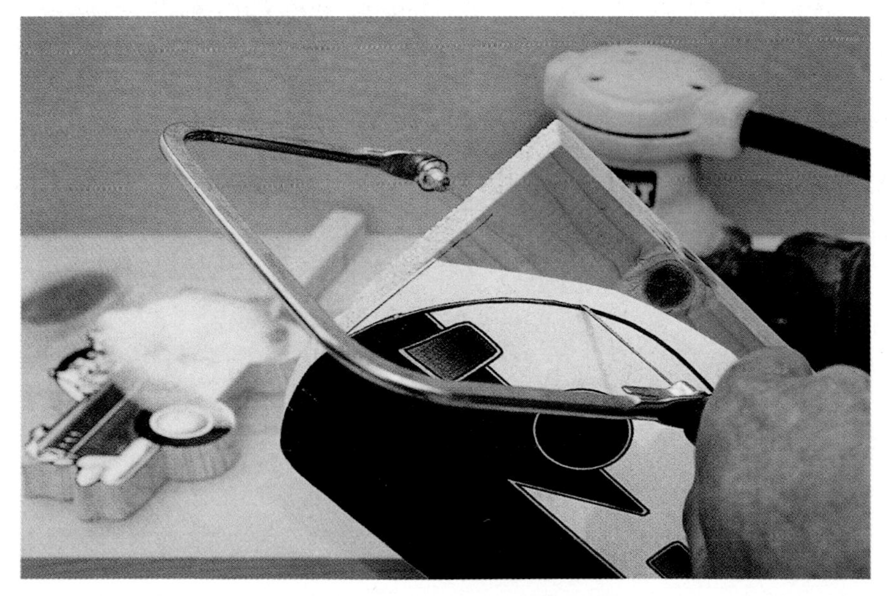

Cut out the car and trailer along the pattern lines, bypassing areas the blade won't easily reach.

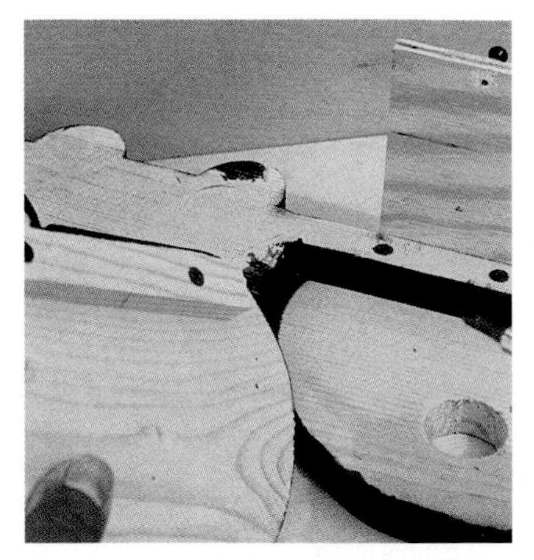
Align the car and trailer graphics and attach the car tongue with glue and drywall screws.

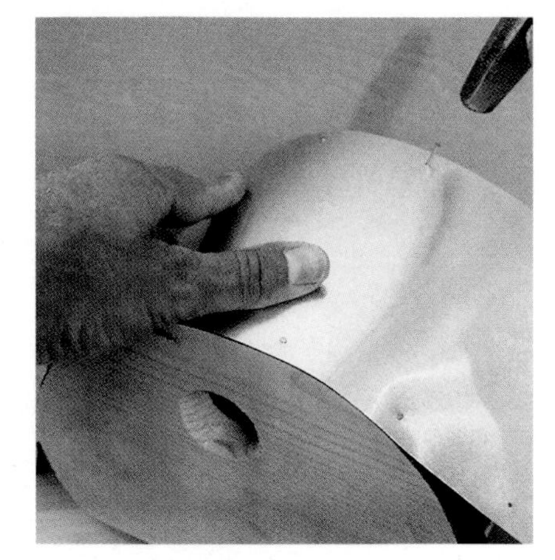
Fasten the flashing with ½-inch brads spaced 2 inches apart and ⅜ inch in from the edges.

BUILD THE TRAILER FRAME

Draw guidelines ¼ inch up from the bottom of each trailer wall to align the car's tongue to the front trailer wall and the cleat to the rear wall. The tongue and the cleat support the floor and align the trailer walls.

Checking that the car and trailer graphics line up, attach the car tongue, as shown above, and the cleat with glue and two drywall screws driven through them into the trailer walls.

Peel off the black-and-white pattern and sand the surfaces smooth.

Fasten the floor to the cleats with drywall screws.

ATTACH THE FLASHING

Drill 1⁄16-inch holes 2 inches apart and ⅜ inch in from each edge of the flashing. Mark and cut a notch for the car tongue so that the flashing will extend below the trailer floor about a half-inch, then fold this piece up inside.

Working from the front of the trailer to the back, fasten the flashing with ½-inch brads, as shown above right, making sure the flashing is flush with both walls of the trailer. When you reach the rear, bend the flashing under the trailer an inch or so, cut it, and nail in place.

Nail on the prepainted tail lights.

AFFIX THE COLOR GRAPHICS

Trim the color graphics to about ¼ inch outside the cutting lines, then cut exactly to the line along the bottoms and around the wheels.

Apply contact cement to the wood car and trailer fronts and to the underside of the color graphics. When the cement has dried, after 10 to 15 minutes, align the graphics at the bottoms and press in place. Burnish down with your fingers through an old T-shirt or other soft cloth, working from the inside out. Finally, use a razor knife to carefully trim away the excess paper, as shown below.

Trace around all edges with a black marker to cover the white edge of the cut paper.

Spray a final coat of satin polyurethane on the finished product.

MOUNT YOUR MOBILE HOME

Since it's designed to be seen from one side only, Route 66 looks best when fence or wall mounted. Working through the entry hole, mount the finished house with a screw driven through the rear wall. ➤

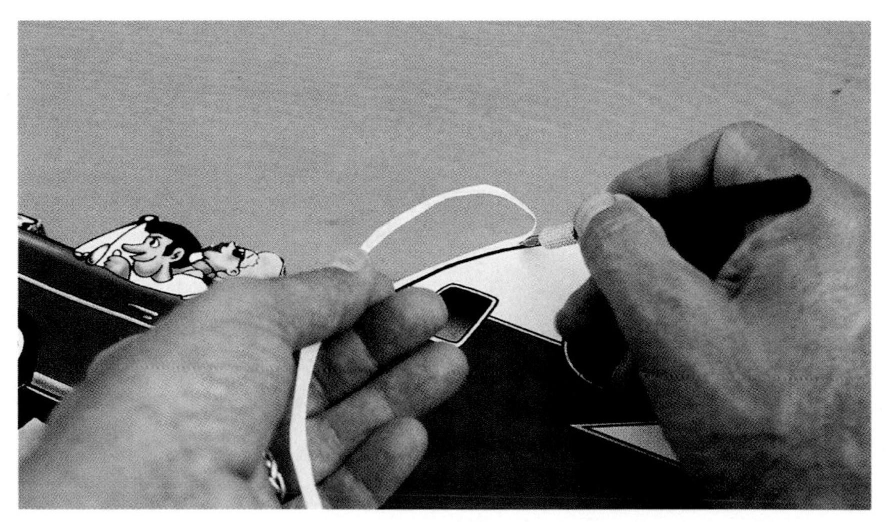
After cementing and burnishing the graphics onto the car and trailer, trim away all excess paper.

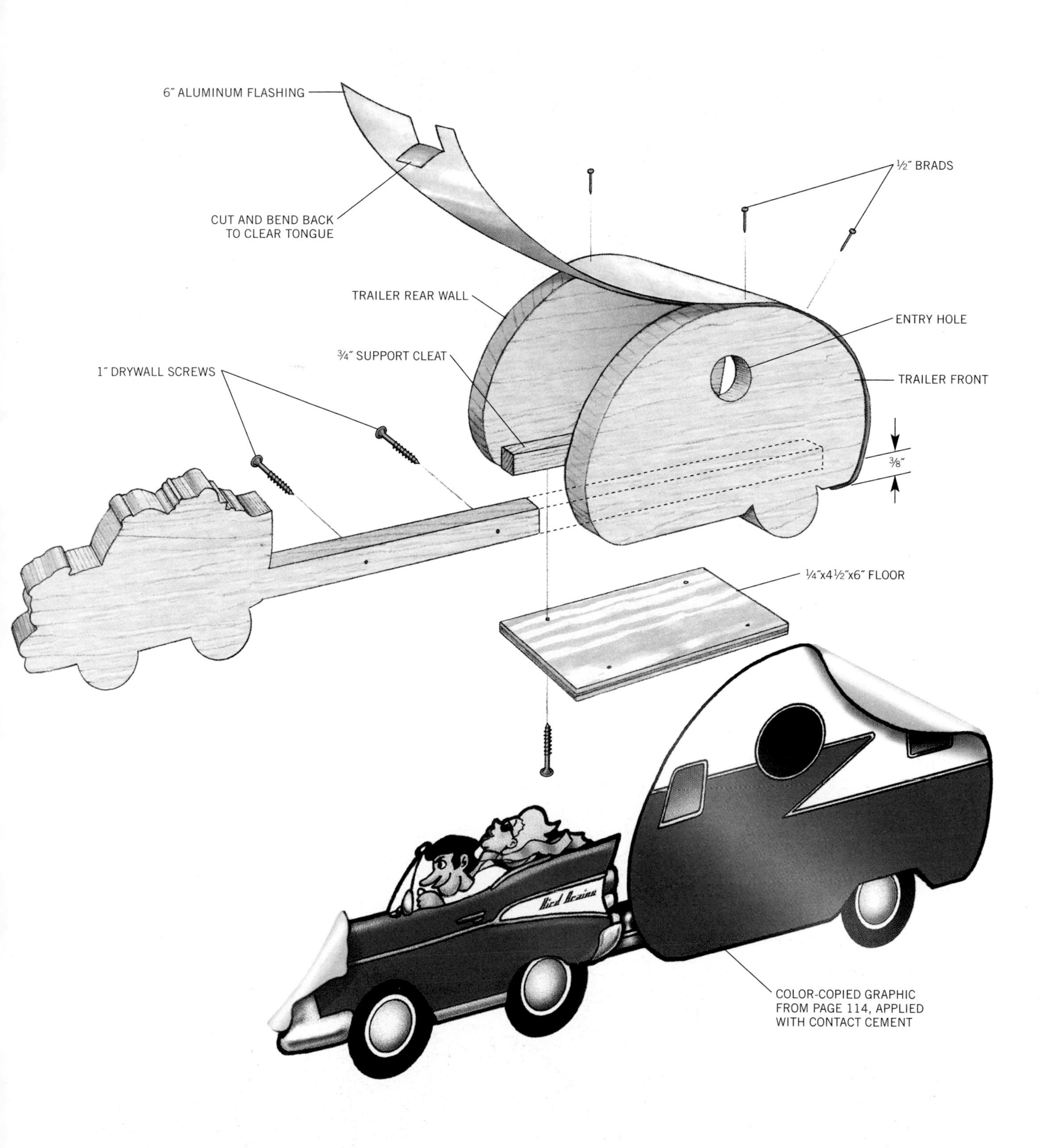
6″ ALUMINUM FLASHING
CUT AND BEND BACK TO CLEAR TONGUE
½″ BRADS
TRAILER REAR WALL
ENTRY HOLE
¾″ SUPPORT CLEAT
1″ DRYWALL SCREWS
TRAILER FRONT
⅜″
¼″x4½″x6″ FLOOR
COLOR-COPIED GRAPHIC FROM PAGE 114, APPLIED WITH CONTACT CEMENT

ROUTE 66 PATTERN & GRAPHIC Actual Size

ARTWORK BY PADDY MORRISSEY

Little Village

This striking multi-unit condo will add plenty of visual interest to any garden, but it's also made to order for purple martins.

To attract residents to the "village," the eight units and their doorways are sized precisely—each floor is 6 inches square, and the entries are large and low. The house also must perch atop a tall pole yet be easily accessible for nest checks, it must be well-ventilated, and it needs to be light in color. We've provided for all of these requirements in our instructions. ➤

MATERIALS

- 1-by-12 pine or other softwood: 3 feet
- 1-by-10 pine or other softwood: 2 feet
- 1-by-8 pine or other softwood: 20 feet
- 1-by-6 pine or other softwood: 3 feet
- 1-by-4 pine or other softwood: 7 feet
- 1-by-3 pine or other softwood: 2 feet
- 1-by-2 pine or other softwood: 3 feet
- 1½-inch outdoor screws
- 3d galvanized finishing nails
- 2-inch-by-¼-inch bolts with nuts and two washers each: 2
- Exterior wood glue
- 1½-inch galvanized hinges: 3 pairs
- Small screen door hooks: 2
- Half-turn buttons: 2
- Fine sandpaper
- Translucent deck finish, thinned paint, or whitewash: white or pale gray

OPTIONAL FOR POLE MOUNT: Two ½-inch pipe supports; one ¼-by-2-inch eyebolt with nut and washer; one 5⁄16-by-1-inch eyebolt with nut and washer; 15 to 18 feet of 1¼-inch (i.d.) steel pipe; concrete for a footing; and a single pulley, S-hook, tie-off, and rope.

TOOLS

- Basic hand tools
- Jigsaw, coping saw, band saw, or scroll saw
- Electric drill, bits, and hole saw for entry holes

OPTIONAL: Table saw, circular saw, electric sander

Despite its highly articulated facade, this is not a tough project. You mostly crosscut standard lumber sizes, then screw the parts together. To work quickly, a circular saw or table saw is helpful, but a jigsaw will do the job.

Although the front might seem to require a lot of measuring and layout, it really doesn't. You just use a combination square—and often the boards themselves—to mark angles and transfer dimensions from one part to another. In fact, since the widths of rough boards can vary considerably, you'll be measuring empirically and will seldom even touch the tape measure.

PREPARE FRONTS & BACKS

Using the square, mark a 45-degree line beginning 8 inches from the bottom of a 1 by 8 and cut piece A1.

Next, match the angled top of A1 with the angled cut on the board, scribe the bottom of A1, and cut to create A2.

The top of module A sets the lower edge of module B/C. To be sure they'll fit accurately, use the combination square to mark a 45-degree line at the top of the 1 by 8, then align A1's longer edge with the line you just drew. With the square, mark a line on the board along the bottom edge of A1.

Cut out this piece (B1), then use it as a template to make three more (B2, C1, and C2).

Use the combination square to mark the entry holes and drill ⅛-inch pilot holes at the center of each. Cut the entry hole in B1 with a hole saw, then use B1 as a guide to drill matching holes in pieces A1 and C1 as shown at bottom left.

With a jigsaw or coping saw, make cutouts for the house extensions in A1 and C1.

PREPARE SIDES & FLOORS

Use A1 as a guide for cutting sides D and E, and use B1 as a guide for cutting sides G.

Cut side D to a 7¾-inch length from 1 by 10. Cut side E from 1 by 10 so that its height exactly matches the long edge of A1 and bevel the top cut to match the angle.

Mark the entry holes, drill pilot holes, then cut them with a 2-inch or 2⅛-inch hole saw.

Fasten house extension A1 to module A with screws, then nail the roof onto the extension.

Cut slots to allow air to flow from the left-hand module up into the right.

Nail the B1 assembly to dividers I and J, angling the nails slightly.

Cut sides G from the 1 by 8 so the height of these pieces is ¼ inch shorter than the short edge of B1.

Align side E with one side G and drill ¼-inch holes through both boards 3 inches from each end and centered side to side.

Cut floors F from 1 by 6 so that their length matches the width of sides D and E.

Cut floors H from 1 by 8 so that their length matches the combined width of B1 and C1 minus the thicknesses of two boards (this should be 1½ inches).

From 1 by 8, cut dividers I to a length of 6 inches.

BUILD THE LEFT-HAND MODULE

Drill ⅜-inch drain holes in floors F.

Nail together sides D and E and floors F. Set one floor flush with the bottom, the other so there is a 6-inch space between floors (use dividers I to set the spacing).

Cut out house extension parts a, b, and c. Cut the entry hole in face a, then nail a, b, and c together.

Fasten this assembly to A1, driving the screws from behind, then nail roof pieces d and e to the house extension.

Nail on a small "eyebrow" above the top hole.

BUILD THE RIGHT-HAND FACADES

Cut out B1 facade extension a and shelves b (to match the width of a). Screw shelves b to a. Screw this assembly to B1, driving screws from behind through a and into the shelves.

Using the holes in B1 as a guide, cut entry holes in this assembly by boring halfway through from behind, then boring from the front once the pilot bit breaks through.

Similarly, cut and build the extension to C1.

ASSEMBLE RIGHT-HAND SHELVES & FLOORS

Drill ⅜-inch drain holes in all floors H where indicated in the illustration on page 119.

Center and screw two dividers I to two floors H. Screw one of these assemblies to uprights G, then attach the other, making sure it's level.

Place B1 in position and measure the distance from the top of the second floor to the top of B1. Cut divider J to this measurement minus ½ inch. Screw J to the remaining floor H and screw the assembly to sides G.

Toenail down through floors H into dividers I, in front and back.

ASSEMBLE THE MODULES

Bolt the left-hand module to the right-hand module with the ¼-inch bolts, nuts, and washers.

Cut vent slots as shown at top left to allow air to flow upward from the left-hand module to the top floor of the right-hand module. ➤

To add the upper pipe strap, screw the left side through B2 into divider J, then bolt it.

Drill overlapping 1¼-inch holes inside the ventilator "footprint" to form a figure 8.

ADD THE RIGHT-HAND FACADES

Nail the B1 facade to side G and floors H. Nail B1 to dividers I and J, angling the nails slightly as shown on page 117.

Similarly, nail the C1 facade assembly in place.

ADD THE REAR PANELS

Attach A2, B2, and C2 to the house with hinges, hooks, and turn buttons.

Cut rear panel B2 lengthwise so that the taller piece is just wide enough to mount the pipe supports, about 4 inches. Fasten the taller piece with screws into shelves H.

To add the pipe straps, screw the bottom strap through the fixed part of B2 into the lowest shelf H. Screw the left side of the top strap through B2, angling the screw into divider J; bolt the right side to B2 with the 1-inch bolt, as shown above.

For access to the center units, hinge and "button" the other half of B2 as you did A2 and C2.

BUILD THE VENTILATOR

From 1-by-2 and 1-by-4 lumber, nail together a 10-inch-long box. Measure the 4-inch-high wall in the center of one side, then use the combination square to mark the two 45-degree gable lines at the top and the 45-degree cutoff line at the bottom. Make these cuts with a handsaw. Drill the vent holes. Cut and nail on the roof pieces.

ADD THE ROOF & VENTILATOR

Measure and cut the left-side roof so that it reaches from the peak to an inch beyond left side D. Position this piece flush with the back panels and screw to the house, then measure from its upper edge to an inch beyond right side G. Cut the right-side roof to this measurement and screw to the right-hand module.

Hold the ventilator in position on the roof, using the combination square to position the ventilator so that its roof line matches the pitch of the right-side roof, and centering it front to back. Trace around the ventilator base, marking its position on the roof.
Set the ventilator aside and drill four ⅛-inch pilot holes where shown in the illustration opposite. Be sure these holes are perfectly vertical. Drill 1¼-inch ventilation holes inside the ventilator "footprint" as shown in the photo near left. Remove the left-side roof and screw the ventilator in place; then replace the roof.

Finish the completed house with a wash of deck finish, thinned white paint, or whitewash.

MOUNTING NOTES

To attract purple martins, mount the house on a 15-foot pole running through the pipe supports. Regular nest checks are recommended, so you must be able to easily raise and lower the house. To facilitate this, attach a 5⁄16-by-1-inch eyebolt to the roof, centered on the pipe supports, and another through the pole at the top; attach a pulley to this one with an S hook. Haul the house up the pole with a rope, securing the rope end to a tie-off at the bottom of the pole. The pole should be mounted two to three feet deep in concrete. For important information on pole location, plus more on purple martins and how to successfully attract them, contact the Purple Martin Conservation Association, or see its Web site at www.purplemartin.org.

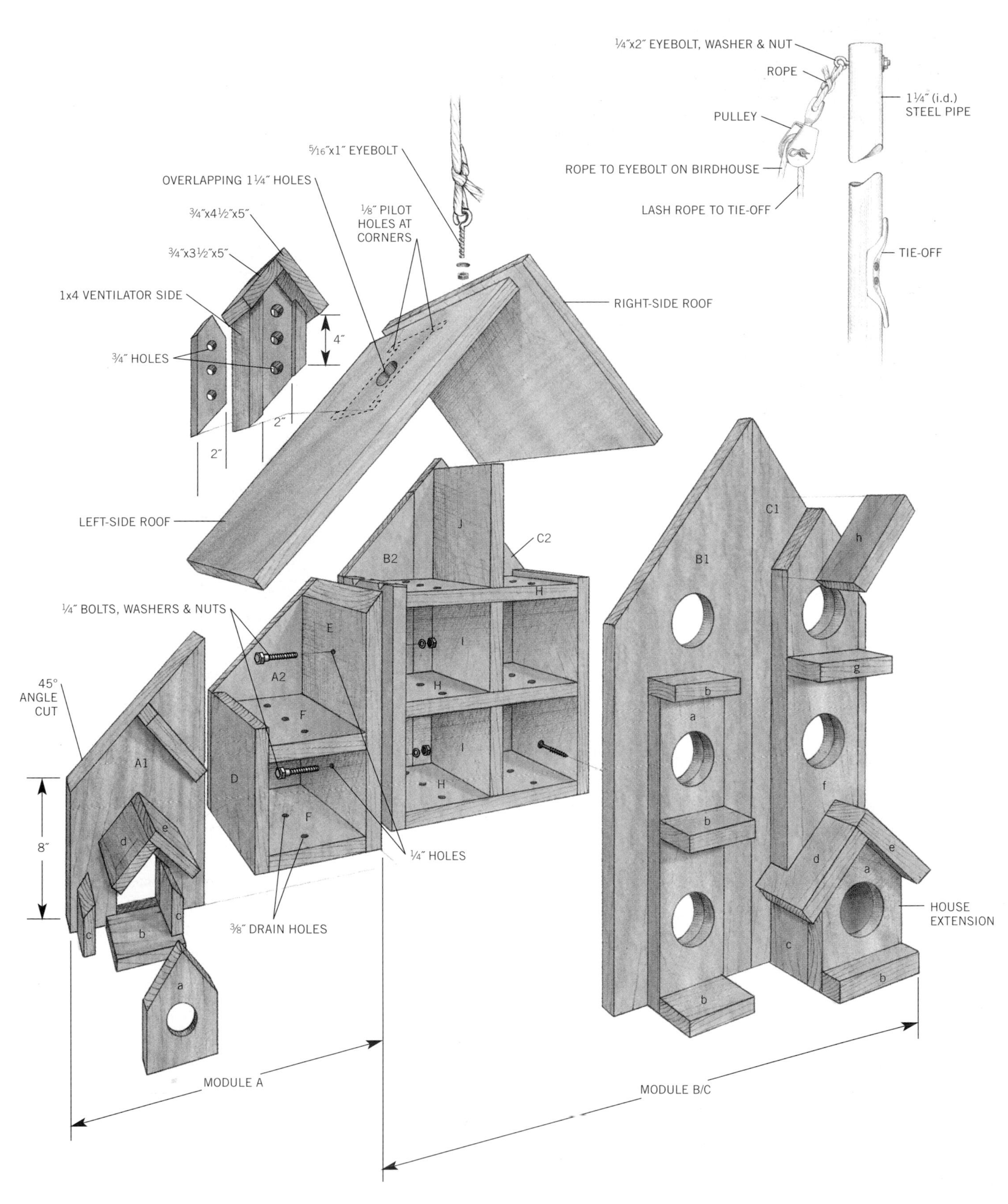
¼″x2″ EYEBOLT, WASHER & NUT
ROPE
PULLEY
1¼″ (i.d.)
STEEL PIPE
ROPE TO EYEBOLT ON BIRDHOUSE
LASH ROPE TO TIE-OFF
TIE-OFF
5⁄16″x1″ EYEBOLT
OVERLAPPING 1¼″ HOLES
⅛″ PILOT
HOLES AT
CORNERS
¾″x4½″x5″
¾″x3½″x5″
1x4 VENTILATOR SIDE
RIGHT-SIDE ROOF
4″
¾″ HOLES
2″
2″
LEFT-SIDE ROOF
J
C2
B2
H
C1
B1
h
¼″ BOLTS, WASHERS & NUTS
E
I
A2
45°
ANGLE
CUT
H
g
F
b
A1
a
D
I
f
H
8″
b
d
e
F
¼″ HOLES
d
e
a
c
HOUSE
EXTENSION
c
b
⅜″ DRAIN HOLES
c
b
a
b
MODULE A
MODULE B/C

TIPS & TECHNIQUES

Building birdhouses should be a relaxed affair. You needn't be perfect in your work; in fact, "casual" construction usually adds to the charm. Materials can be rough and ready, joints are nearly always simple, and even a fancy birdhouse takes only a couple of afternoons to build.

Birdhouse building is also opportunistic. You can often build from scrap—a great way to rid your shop of cutoffs, odd boards, and leftover materials. Indeed, some of the most charming houses come about this way. We've suggested a few projects using such materials as driftwood, moss, and seashells, but plan to let your own collection of flotsam and jetsam inspire you.

Think of the projects in this book as starting points for your own ideas. In many cases, you can adapt them as you see fit, adding the roof of one to the walls of another, swapping finishes, modifying designs to finally create your own originals.

Following is a guide to basic techniques, with notes on the materials and methods used in the projects contained in this book.

ABOVE: Redwood (shown here) and cedar offer natural resistance to decay, which makes them ideal for outdoor birdhouses.

BELOW: Using a wire wheel, erode the soft wood between annular rings of redwood or cedar to create interesting texture.

CHOOSING MATERIALS

What are some of the most common building materials? Here are a few.

PINE This is the best choice for birdhouses that will be stained or painted since its pale hue makes an excellent background for color. Widely available, 1-by pine is easy to cut and sand, and inexpensive grades are fine for birdhouses. Although it's sturdy enough to leave unfinished, pine won't last as long this way as redwood or cedar.

Readily available, inexpensive, and easy to tool, pine is the most popular wood for building birdhouses.

REDWOOD & CEDAR These are your best choices for birdhouses that will be exposed to weather year-round, year in and year out. These naturally rot-resistant species can be left unfinished, though they also readily take clear finishes and paint. With their prominent annular rings, they lend themselves to wire-wheel texturing. Choose "surfaced" lumber for a smooth look; "rough" for an attractively shaggy appearance.

PRESSURE-TREATED WOOD Do not use it for birdhouses; it's a safety hazard in the workshop and toxic to the birds.

FIR PLYWOOD Rated for outdoor exposure (CDX and other exterior grades), it works well for birdhouses, especially if they won't be left out all year long. Use plywood for projects where a thinner material is required for looks or where it will be covered by a weatherproof material. Unless plywood is very well sealed against the elements, its edges will eventually delaminate.

DOOR SKIN This thin, inexpensive, flexible hardwood plywood normally used for cladding hollow-core doors is the only material that readily allows compound curves. Seal it well with polyurethane or paint, and even then don't plan to leave your project outside year-round.

SHINGLES & SHAKES Cedar shingles are great for birdhouse roofs and make excellent wall cladding, too. It's easy to

Plywood rated for outdoor exposure, well sealed, is best for projects where a thin but strong material is required.

Great for roofs and siding, shims made from cedar shingles split to "scale" size are readily available at lumberyards.

Patching compound is wonderfully flexible when wet and, especially when reinforced, hardens to form a durable wall.

make weathertight layers, and a finish is entirely optional. Most home centers sell shims made from cedar shingles, which come knot-free and already split to "scale" width. Alternatively, a single cedar shake can make an entire roof panel. Also consider asphalt shingles. When nailed to 1-by wood, these make excellent roofs.

METAL Copper, galvanized steel, and aluminum are available in sheets and in rolls sold as flashing. These weatherproof materials are great for quick and easy roofs and also make good side walls. Houses made with metal roofs or walls will be subject to wider temperature fluctuations than those made of solid wood, and are better placed out of the sun.

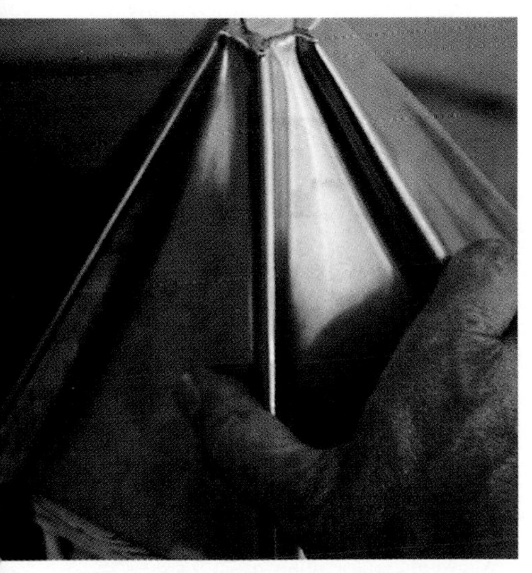

Because they are weatherproof and easy to form, copper (shown here), galvanized steel, and aluminum are excellent for roofing. Mount a metal-roofed birdhouse out of the sun to prevent toasty interior temperatures.

PATCHING COMPOUND Applied to an armature and reinforced with cheesecloth or wire, patching compound (either plaster- or concrete-based) is tremendously flexible and hardens to form a durable wall of almost any form you can imagine. When completely dry, apply several coats of polyurethane or marine varnish for durability outdoors.

GOING ABOUT THE JOB

Many birdhouses, especially those made of wood, are built using conventional woodworking tools and techniques. Following is a closer look at some of the most common procedures.

MEASURING & MARKING Use your tape measure to measure boards for cutting, then use a combination square to mark the cutting lines. Use a sharp pencil or the scriber from your combination square, holding the instrument at a 60-degree angle to the work and marking right where the blade of the square meets the wood.

Plan to cut on the "waste" side of your marks. Since the saw blade consumes wood, don't mark the pieces all at once, which would create cumulative errors. Instead, mark one piece, cut, then mark another, cut, and so on.

In birdhouse building, pieces are often paired (ends, sides, roof panels). Don't measure twice; instead, lay out one piece of a pair, cut it out, then use it as a tracing pattern for its mate. This saves time and ensures a better match.

To locate an entry hole, first draw a center line on one end piece. Following the project drawing or the chart on pages 126–127, measure up from the base along the center line to locate the center of the hole.

When a project requires a pattern, first enlarge it on a copier as specified. Then mount it to the wood with rubber cement or spray adhesive. Be sure to position the pattern so that you'll be able to cut outside the lines.

CUTTING STRAIGHT A basic crosscut saw does a fine job of cutting boards. Since it cuts on the downstroke, mark and cut on the "good" side of your wood. Be sure to support your work in a vise or clamp it to your bench top or a sawhorse.

Power tools are a great aid for any kind of shop work. A jigsaw (saber saw) should be your first power saw. It's great for cutting curves and, with an edge guide, also works well for the straight cuts needed in birdhouse building. Because the blade cuts on the upstroke, mark and cut on the back side of the wood. To start a cutout in a panel or when cutting inside corners, first drill a pilot hole.

A circular saw is a fine workhorse tool for straight cuts, especially in plywood sheets; it's also very useful for larger birdhouse projects. For ripping, use the saw's edge guide where possible. Work on the back side of the material, sighting the cutout line in the saw's gunsight notch.

A table saw or radial arm saw is handy, particularly if you're making several birdhouses of the same basic design. Accurate repeatability is the main feature of these tools. Set up so that you cut all the identical parts at once. With a table saw, mark and cut on the top surface of the work; with a radial arm saw, mark crosscuts on top, rip cuts on the back.

CUTTING CURVES Most curved cuts in this book can be done with a coping saw. Support your work in a vise or clamp it to your bench top or sawhorse, reclamping as needed to follow the curve. Mark and cut on the "good" side of the wood. As noted above, a jigsaw makes a project much easier; don't forget to mark and cut on the back side.

FASTENING The projects in this book use only butt and face joints, usually either nailed or screwed and often backed up with glue. Here are some notes on materials and methods:

- Screws are your best bet for birdhouses that must stand up to years of weather exposure. With their easy-driving, tight-holding design, modern outdoor screws (also known as deck screws) are a wonderful improvement over traditional wood screws and perfect for power driving. Where appearance matters, we've also specified brass wood screws; drive these with a hand screwdriver. Drywall screws are also useful, but they will rust in time, so use them only where they won't be visible. Although outdoor and drywall screws don't require pilot holes, we suggest you always drill them, just to be sure you get the screw in the right place. In certain projects, you'll conceal screw heads in counterbored holes capped with screw buttons, readily available at hardware stores.

Screw heads can be easily concealed by counterboring the holes and capping the sunken screws with wooden buttons.

- Galvanized finish nails—usually 3d, or "three-penny" (1¼-inch)—are the principal nails used in these projects. Always drill 1/16-inch pilot holes an inch or so deep. With a hammer, drive nails nearly flush, then countersink slightly with a nailset. Where extra grip is needed, we've specified box nails. These have slimmer shanks than common nails, with wide heads that are just right for resisting spring-back pressure. Again, pilot holes are a must.

- Brads are essentially miniature nails, and escutcheon pins, with their round

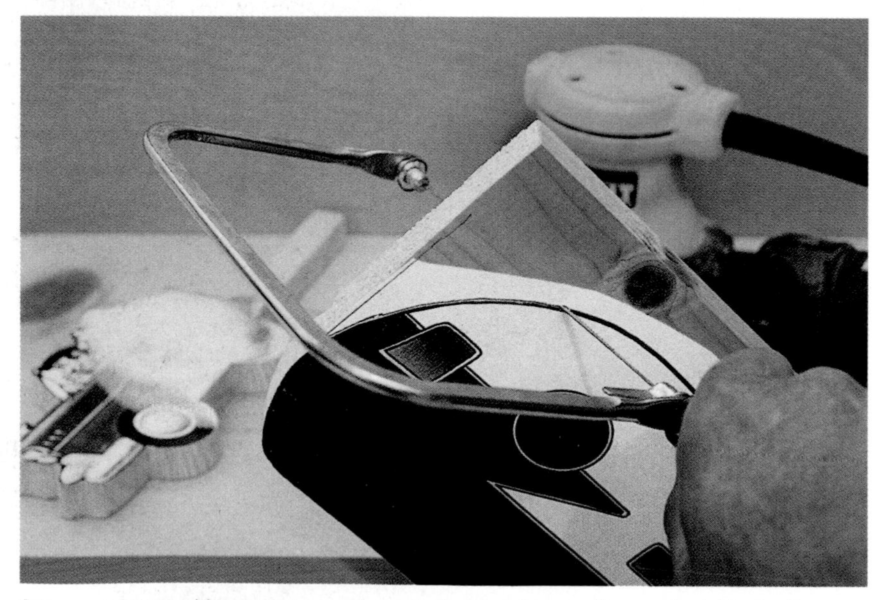

Curves can be cut with a coping saw; when a project requires a pattern, cut outside the lines.

Wood glue serves as a backup for mechanical fasteners and as an adherent for projects requiring decoupage.

Silicone can bond two materials together or seal joints between materials; in some cases, it is the only way two pieces can be joined.

Though not essential, a belt or random-orbit sander comes in handy for projects requiring considerable sanding.

heads, are a variant. We've used these when fastening metal and other thin materials. Start these fasteners with a pair of pliers, then tap home with a tack hammer.

■ Hot glue, though poor at forming a weather-resistant bond, is perfect for those times you need a third hand. It's also great for quickly assembling indoors-only birdhouses. Make sure to use the yellow glue sticks specified for woodworking.

■ Wood glue is helpful but only as a backup to mechanical fasteners or for use in a project requiring decoupage. Any "carpenter's" (aliphatic resin) glue will do, but be sure it's for exterior use.

■ Silicone adhesive/sealant forms a durable, flexible, all-weather bond, and in some cases is the only way two pieces could be joined. Be sure to buy silicone rated for outdoor use.

SANDING Birdhouses don't require much surface preparation. If you're sanding at all, start with 100- or 120-grit, then make another pass with 180- or 200-grit. A rubber or wood sanding block speeds the work and helps prevent gouges. Certain projects benefit from power sanding. Here, a belt sander or random-orbit sander comes in handy. Always dust well after sanding with a tack cloth, shop vacuum, or both.

COLORED & SPECIALTY FINISHES

A great finish is usually the critical finishing touch to a successful birdhouse. Not only does a finish protect the birdhouse, it usually gives it its visual style.

OIL- & WATER-BASED ENAMELS Widely available in a rainbow of colors, enamels provide for quick and easy paint jobs. For the best look, sand first, then use a flat white undercoat before applying the finish colors.

TEMPERA PAINTS Great for easy "painterly" effects, these paints can be mixed very freely and still result in bright colors (not always the case with enamels). Best of all, they're forgiving: if you goof, just sponge off the area and start over. Since tempera is water-based, you must topcoat with polyurethane or another clear finish to preserve your work.

STAINS Whether water- or oil-based, stains let you change the tone of wood without hiding the grain. You must topcoat with a clear finish when dry. Water-based stains may raise the grain of the wood; if they do, sand lightly with fine paper before topcoating.

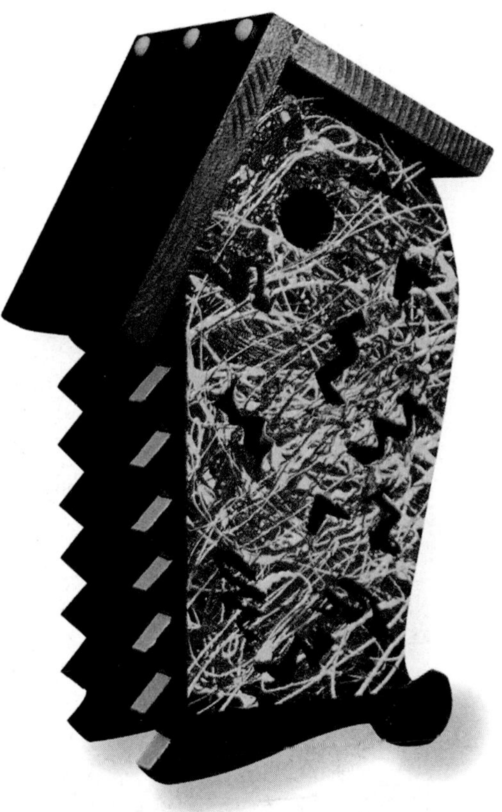
Oil-based enamels provide a long-lasting finish in a broad palette of colors.

Tempera paints are very forgiving because they are water-based, but to endure they must be given a clear top coat.

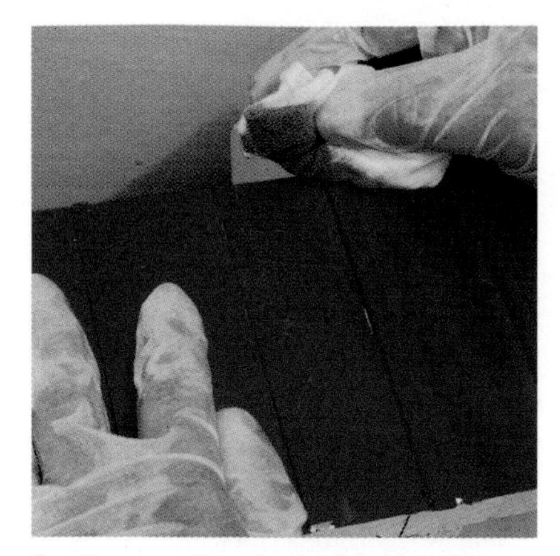

Creating an antiqued paint finish requires nothing more than wiping with a rag lightly dampened in stain.

DYES Leather dyes, readily available at leather working crafts stores, look terrific on wood, especially pine. They coat with vivid color but without hiding the grain. They come in every hue and must be topcoated with a clear finish to preserve the color. Aniline dyes, available at specialty woodworking shops, work the same way but are more difficult to find.

ANTIQUE, WASH & DISTRESSED FINISHES To antique a paint job, wipe it with a rag barely dampened in stain. To create a wash finish, which looks particularly good on rough wood, apply thinned paint with a rag or chip brush. To texture wood, use a wire wheel. If you burn the surface first, you'll get a high-relief, Japanese-style finish.

ART PAPER Art papers are widely available at art supply and specialty stores. You can create a world of unique surface treatments with them, and no two projects will be exactly alike. Decoupage onto wood using thinned wood glue, then topcoat with plenty of polyurethane.

Tile grout will affix lightweight materials, such as shells, driftwood, and pebbles, to plaster.

PLASTER & GROUT Patching plaster is perfect as a finish for Tudor-, Mediterranean-, or Southwest-style birdhouses. Tile grout is excellent for bonding shells, driftwood, and pebbles to a plaster wall. Protect the finished surface with polyurethane or other clear finish.

CLEAR FINISHES

Clear finishes can be applied directly on wood or other materials, or used as a protective coating for colored and specialty finishes.

POLYURETHANE Apply several coats, sprayed or brushed, to materials specified for exterior use to give your projects a durable, weather-resistant finish. Choose satin "poly" for a natural look, gloss for a high shine. We found the spray versions to be a fast, fuss-free way to finish the irregular surfaces of a birdhouse. Because it dries fast, you can add all the coats you need in just a half hour or so.

DECK FINISHES Clear deck finish is especially suited to unstained wood, deepening the natural tones and protecting the surface. For more color, try semitransparent colored finishes.

MARINE (SPAR) VARNISH The ultimate in protection against the elements, marine varnish is available in satin and gloss. It adds a honey tone to projects, making them almost glow. If the gloss is too glossy for your taste, use steel wool to dull the finish a bit.

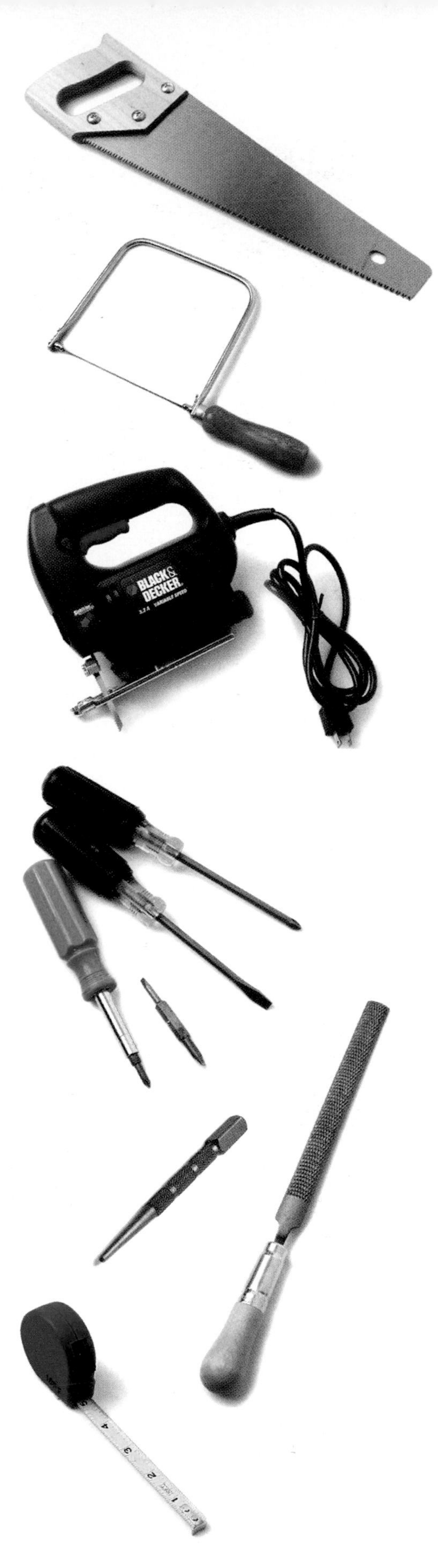

A BASIC SET OF HAND TOOLS

COMBINATION SQUARE Essential for birdhouse building, it lets you quickly mark 90-degree and 45-degree crosscuts, the most common you'll make.

SAWS A basic crosscut saw works fine for straight cuts, a coping saw for curves. For birdhouse building, an electric jigsaw (saber saw) is ideal for both.

UTILITY KNIFE Great for trimming and detail work, it's also useful for cutting the paper and cloth used in some of the projects.

DRILL & BITS Nowadays, an electric drill has become a stock tool. For most projects, you'll need a basic set of twist bits (1/16-inch through 3/8-inch), plus a spade bit or hole saw of a size to bore the desired entry hole.

SCREWDRIVERS You'll need a #2 Phillips bit to drive the outdoor screws often specified in this book, plus a straight bit for some of the other screws. A four- or six-in-one screwdriver is a good choice, as is a battery-operated drill with driver bits.

HAMMERS A standard 16-ounce nailing or framing hammer is just right for birdhouses; a tack hammer comes in handy for driving brads and escutcheon pins.

NAILSET You'll need one or more of these for countersinking the finish nails specified in many of this book's projects.

RASP Handy for roughing out shapes, chamfering, and distressing surfaces, it removes stock quickly, leaving a rough surface.

PLIERS Perfect for twisting up wire hangers or removing errant fasteners, they're handy any time you need a "bionic hand."

TAPE MEASURE Great for marking cutoffs along a board's edge; mark the actual crosscut lines with a combination square.

Building for the Birds

It is a curious fact of nature that only 13 percent of the bird population is drawn to birdhouses—despite the success rate of cavity nesters far outstripping that of non-nesters. Of course, birds tend to be picky about their homes; make the entry hole too large or the interior dimension too small, and a prospective tenant may turn out to be only the briefest of visitors. Below are some of the most common species in North America along with their room—and board—requirements.

SPECIES	BIRD	LOCALE	INTERIOR SIZE (INCHES)
BLUEBIRD	Eastern	East of Great Plains states	4x4–5x5
	Mountain	Rocky Mountain region	5x5–5½x5½
	Western	West of the Rocky Mountains	5x5
CHICKADEE	Black-capped	Northern U.S.	4x4–5x5
	Carolina	Southeastern U.S.	4x4–5x5
	Chestnut-backed	Coastal belt from Alaska to Central California	4x4–5x5
	Mountain	Western U.S. from 6,000 to 11,000 feet	4x4–5x5
FINCH	House	All of continental U.S.	4x4–6x6
FLYCATCHER	Ash-throated	Pacific Northwestern and Southwestern U.S.	4x4–6x6
	Great-crested	East of the Rocky Mountains	4x4–6x6
MARTIN	Purple	East of the Rocky Mountains, West Coast	6x6
NUTHATCH	Red-breasted	All of North America	4x4–5x5
	White-breasted	Eastern and Western U.S.	4x4–5x5
OWL	Screech	All of continental U.S.	6x6–8x8
SPARROW	House	All of North America	4x4–5x5
STARLING	European	All of North America	5x5–6x6
SWALLOW	Tree	All of North America	4x4–5x5
	Violet-green	Western North America	4x4–5x5
TITMOUSE	Plain	Oregon south and west to Texas	4x4–5x5
	Tufted	East of the Rocky Mountains	4x4–5x5
WARBLER	Prothonotary	East of the Rocky Mountains	4x4–5x5
WOODPECKER	Downy	All of North America	3x3–4x4
	Hairy	All of North America	5x5–6x6
	Northern flicker	All of North America	6x6–8x8
	Red-bellied, Red-headed	East of the Rocky Mountains	5x5–6x6
WREN	Bewick's	Southern U.S.	4x4–5x5
	Carolina	East of the Rocky Mountains	4x4–5x5
	House	All of North America	4x4–5x5

HEIGHT OF BOX (INCHES)	ENTRANCE DIAMETER (INCHES)	HEIGHT OF ENTRANCE (INCHES)	HEIGHT ABOVE GROUND (FEET)	FOOD
8–12	1½	6–7	5–10	Wild fruits
11–12	1⁹⁄₁₆	6–7	5–10	Seeds and berries
8–12	1½–1⁹⁄₁₆	6–7	5–10	72% insects/28% wild fruits
8–12	1⅛–1½	6–8	5–15	70% insects/30% wild fruits
8–12	1⅛–1½	6–8	6–15	70% insects/30% wild fruits
8–12	1⅛–1½	6–8	6–15	65% insects/35% seeds and fruits
8–12	1⅛–1½	6–8	6–15	98% insects/2% seeds and fruits
6–12	1⅜–2	4–7	8–12	Fruits and seeds
8–12	1½–2½	6–7	8–20	92% insects/8% fruits
8–12	1½–2½	6–8	8–20	94% insects/6% wild fruits
6	2–2½	1	15–20	Insects
8–12	1⅛–1½	6–8	5–20	Seeds and insects
9–12	1⅛–1½	6–7	5–20	Insects and seeds
12–18	2½–4	9–12	10–30	Mice and insects
8–12	1³⁄₁₆–2	6–8	4–12	Insects, grain, and seeds
13–20	1⅝–4	6–16	10–25	57% insects/43% fruits
9–12	1¼–1½	1–7	5–15	Seeds and berries
6–12	1¼–1½	1–7	5–15	Insects
8–12	1¼–1½	6–8	6–15	57% plant matter/43% insects
8–12	1¼–1½	6–8	6–15	82%–89% insects/11%–18% seeds and berries
8–12	1¼–1½	5–7	4–12	Insects
8–14	1¼–1½	6–14	6–20	75% insects/25% fruits
12–16	1½–2¾	9–14	12–20	80% insects/20% fruits and nuts
14–24	2–3	10–20	6–20	60% insects/40% seeds, grain, and fruits
12–16	1¾–2¾	9–14	12–20	Insects, grain, nuts, and fruits
6–12	1–1½	1–7	6–10	97% insects/3% plants
6–12	1–1½	1–7	6–10	94% insects/6% seeds
6–12	1–1½	1–7	6–10	98% insects/2% plants

RESOURCES & CREDITS

THE BIRDHOUSE STUDIO
R.R.#1, Minden
Ontario, Canada K0M 2K0
(705) 286-6535
www.birdhousestudio.ca
Created by John and Lindsay Beaudry, the Birdhouse Studio's custom birdhouses are made from 1-inch clean pine and topped with hand-milled cedar shake roofs. All are fully functional. Prices start at $225.

THE BIRDHOUSING COMPANY
679 Darlington Circle
Atlanta, GA 30305
(404) 231-4764
(404) 869-1967 (fax)
www.birdhousing.com
Created by Peggi Carman, the Birdhousing Company's birdhouses are made from either white Southern pine or cedar. All paints used are outdoor latex; interiors are left natural. Prices for stock birdhouses range from $28 to $55.

MIKE DILLON
11775 Harbour Reach Drive
Mukilteo, WA 98275
(425) 493-8309
(425) 493-8310 (fax)
www.dillonworks.com
Mike Dillon's birdhouses are art pieces inspired by a variety of materials, abandoning the traditional rules of birdhouse construction. Dillon's designs can be found in *The Art of the Birdhouse: Flights of Fancy* (Andrews and McMeel, 1997) and in *The Great Birdhouse Book* (Sterling Publishing Co., Inc., 1999).

DUKE BIRDHOUSE, INC.
Rt. 8, Box 37
Andalusia, AL 36420
(334) 222-9633
www.dukebirdhouse.com
Greg Duke's birdhouses are fashioned from 1-by-4 tongue-and-groove heart pine, door panels, and wide base molding "harvested" from old houses and schools. He builds primarily for display yet all houses are water-sealed for exterior use. Prices run $150 to $750 and up.

ERICKSON BIRDHOUSE COMPANY
1140 Elizabeth Avenue, Suite #1
Lancaster, PA 17601
(800) 382-2473 or (717) 397-2266
www.bird-houses.com
Created by Eric Berman, Erickson birdhouses are hand-crafted from old and new wood, assembled with copper and brass fittings, and clad with a verdigris copper or rusted-tin roof. Side walls open for easy cleanout and all openings measure 1¼ inches. Prices range from $70 to $150.

PATRICIA KLAMSER
308 20th Avenue South
Seattle, WA 98144
(206) 322-8819
Patricia Klamser's award-winning birdhouses, inspired by a Japanese sensibility, are carried in more than 30 galleries nationwide. Though they are suitable for indoor or outdoor use, most buyers consider them collectibles. Prices range from $300 to $500.

CREDITS

PAGE 4 Design: B. Leader; Photography: Norman A. Plate
PAGE 5 Photography: Allan Mandell
PAGES 1–3; PAGE 6; PAGES 20–125 Design and photography: Scott Fitzgerrell
PAGE 7 TOP Design: Linda Terhark; Photography: David Wakely
PAGE 7 BOTTOM Photography: Saxon Holt
PAGE 8 BOTTOM LEFT; PAGE 9 TOP LEFT; PAGE 9 TOP RIGHT Photography: Jean-Claude Hurni
PAGE 8 BOTTOM RIGHT Photography: Roger Foley
PAGE 9 BOTTOM Photography: Southern Progress Corporation
PAGE 10 Photography: Noel Barnhurst
PAGE 11 TOP Design and photography: Erickson Birdhouse Company
PAGE 11 BOTTOM Photography: Maslowski Photo
PAGE 12, ALL PHOTOS; PAGE 13 TOP LEFT, PAGE 13 TOP RIGHT Design and photography: The Birdhousing Company
PAGE 13 TOP LEFT Design: Kathleen MacIntyre; Photography: Erickson Birdhouse Company
PAGE 14, ALL PHOTOS Design and photography: The Birdhouse Studio
PAGE 15 TOP RIGHT Photography: Deidra Walpole Photography
PAGE 15 BOTTOM; PAGE 16 LEFT; PAGE 19 TOP RIGHT, PAGE 19 BOTTOM RIGHT Design: Mike Dillon; Photography: Jim Linna
PAGES 16–17 Design: Greg Duke. Photography: Van Chaplin
PAGES 18–19 Design and photography: Patricia Klamser